MW00681812

Your Personal
Marketing
Playbook

To Sloane,

Susan Crossman
& Paula Hope

For "Mr. Networker", himself ☺
Paula

Manor House

Library and Archives Canada
Cataloguing in Publication

Title: Your Personal Marketing Playbook / Susan Crossman & Paula Hope.

Names: Crossman, Susan (Susan G.), author. | Hope, Paula, author.

Description: Includes bibliographical references.

Identifiers: Canadiana 20190080329 |

ISBN 9781988058481 (hardcover) |

ISBN 9781988058474 (softcover)

Subjects: LCSH: Business networks. | LCSH: Social networks. |

LCSH: Interpersonal relations.

Classification: LCC HD69.S8 C76 2019 | DDC 650.1/3—dc23

Copyright: 2019 / 220 pages

Cover main art: Trevor Stooke

Published by Manor House Publishing Inc.

452 Cottingham Crescent, Ancaster, Ontario, Canada, L9G 3V6 /905-648-2193 / All rights reserved. www.manor-house-publishing.com

This project has been made possible [in part] by the Government of Canada. « *Ce projet a été rendu possible [en partie] grâce au gouvernement du Canada.*

Funded by the Government of Canada
Financé par le gouvernement du Canada

This book is dedicated to any professional service provider who has ever felt there is more available to them in life and business than they are currently experiencing...and who is on the path to figuring out how to "turn on the business development tap" so greater abundance can flow their way.

May you thrive and succeed in all your endeavours, and may you know the pride that comes from a solid business that is marketed with integrity.

Acknowledgements

From Susan

She has brought countless grace notes and light-bulb moments to the writing of this book and so, first and foremost, I want to thank my co-author and dear friend, Paula Hope. I appreciate her generous heart and unflagging optimism as I've unfurled myself and my business into a future that is continuously evolving, and compelling. My thanks also to publisher Michael Davie and Manor House.

I also want to thank my children, for being the best teachers a person could ever ask for. They warm my heart, expand my outlook and surprise me often.

And, finally, decades ago an intimidating creative genius with an anger management problem took a chance and hired me to become a copywriter for the successful marketing firm he ran. So thanks, also, to Rick Winchell, for giving me my start in marketing.

From Paula

This book was made possible by the patience and understanding of my wonderful co-author, editor, book coach and lovely friend, Susan Crossman. I am so lucky to have her in my life and I thank my stars every day for her.

Speaking of gratitude to special people, I have also been blessed by my birth and blended family members who are always there for me. I want to give a special nod of acknowledgement to my daughter.

Finally, to my clients and friends, I want to thank you for the support and wisdom that you have shared with me over, lo, these many years. I am always grateful to David for growing old with me, "the best *is* yet to be."

TABLE OF CONTENTS

Praise for Your Personal Marketing Playbook

"The perfect recipe for personal marketing on steroids! A practical, real-life guide for building a powerful Referral Content Marketing Plan! Paula and Susan have crafted a masterpiece."

-- **Husam Jandal**, Digital Rainmaker

"Paula Hope and Susan Crossman's new book brings together the pieces of a puzzle that eludes most people and it's the answer you've been seeking."

- **James Burchill**, Coursepreneur™, Producer and Best-selling Author

"I have read every author on the topic of referrals to build my expertise. This book is exceptional... I couldn't put it down! It is engaging and you can apply it to your business immediately."

- **Victoria Trafton**, Referral Expert

Your Personal Marketing Playbook

FOREWORD

Relationships sustain us.

Where would be without our parents, our children, our husbands, wives, significant others, friends, business colleagues, sports friends, neighbours, or casual acquaintances? It is safe to say that without relationships, we would be nowhere.

Mere shells of ourselves.

The same truth applies to the business world. In fact, relationships are the real DNA of the business world.

And, yet, very few business people see their relationships as a personal core asset, one that can be cultivated, nurtured and expanded into a key method of creating ongoing opportunity for themselves, and for everyone they meet.

We've written this book to recognize and honour this most undervalued asset in our business lives. Our goal is to help our readers, our clients, and our network members take advantage of the best asset that they have.

And have fun while doing so!

As experts in the two most important channels for tapping into the full potential of our business relationships, we have joined forces to help our readers grow their relationships by growing themselves, both on- and offline.

Author Susan Crossman is an online marketing consultant who helps her clients develop, manage, and leverage the web-related content they need to grow their business with clarity and authority.

She has already written a highly informative book on the topic, **Content Marketing Made Easy – Why You Need It/How To Do it**. [1]

She has an extensive background as a professional writer and marketer and she is tenaciously focused on helping her clients untangle the often overwhelming task of showing up more powerfully online while leveraging the internet's vast possibilities for revenue generation.

The field of online marketing is changing all the time and Susan is focused on ensuring her clients get involved with it in ways that are aligned with their goals, their interests and their budget.

---

[1] https://amzn.to/2Tf7GPp

Author Paula Hope is a leading referral marketing consultant, certified coach, speaker and trainer who helps talented business professionals become happily booked solid through referrals.

Paula has seen first-hand how powerful referrals can be in the corporate world and now, as a certified coach and trainer, she is focused on assisting professional service providers to exceptional success through their own customized system and plan for creating referrals. She takes great delight in sharing her valuable knowledge and experience with her clients.

Susan was Paula's book coach and editor for her first book, *Stop the Saboteurs: Conquer Negative Thoughts that Hurt Your Revenue and Your Brand.*

And Paula has been a powerful mentor in Susan's own journey towards building and leveraging her network for business success.

Together, in *Your Personal Marketing Playbook*, we explore the plays, or tactics, that a business professional can use to develop his or her social capital, on or off line, to create the revenue they truly deserve – while enjoying their lives.

11

We call this collection of activities "Personal Marketing."

We've developed a formula to help our readers see their opportunity more clearly, and it summarizes our recommended method of combining 100 referral marketing methods with the ever-expanding range of online tactics available today:

Referral Marketing + Content Marketing = Personal Marketing = Success

We hope that you enjoy learning more about your wonderful asset. We also hope that the valuable knowledge in *Your Personal Marketing Playbook* brings you abundance beyond your wildest dreams.

Best wishes for a smooth climb to success!

Susan Crossman
Oakville, Ontario, Canada

Paula Hope
Town of Blue Mountains, Ontario, Canada

Introduction: The Art of Creating Social Capital – On and Offline

The all-important task of mastering the knack of new business development is a big challenge for many professional service providers. We're *told* it's important, and we *know* it's important...but unless we have someone take us by the hand and share everything they know about creating new business, we can sometimes find ourselves floundering.

Sometimes?!

New business development is not something most of us learn at our parents' knees, and it's typically not taught in schools. But it does involve a process that can be learned and conquered.

You may know in your bones that networking is important to this undertaking. And you may have a sense that you're supposed to be doing something-or-other online.

The common ground both arenas share is the fact that your activity, in each, is all about relationships. Creating them, nurturing them, solidifying them, and profiting from them.

Profit from a relationship? Isn't that a cold and calculating thing to do? No, — not if the intention is to generate mutual benefit.

There is a key distinction to be made here between relationships that are strictly transactional, or even slightly predatory, and those that are based in mutual respect, understanding, and goodwill.

This is true in your social world, as well, by the way—have you ever been in a relationship with someone who is always keeping score, in an "I-did-this-for-you-now-you-have-to-do-that-for-me" kind of way? It's unpleasant, isn't it? The same is true in business.

You want to build healthy relationships with the members of your network, ones where you can both flourish and shine.

Making it Rain
So, if you are in charge of new business development for your organization, or if you are an entrepreneur who has to "make it rain," take heart.

This book is designed to share some tried-and-true tips and techniques for creating a personal marketing system that supports you and the people who can add value to your business and, ultimately, to your life.

The thing to remember is that personal marketing, on or offline, is about creating, managing and leveraging your social capital.

So, what is social capital? Would it surprise you to hear that the pundits cannot settle on a definition of this crucial social force? Here is the definition that we use in *Your Personal Marketing Playbook*:

Social capital is the goodwill that you create with members of your network.

That goodwill starts with giving, helping, and developing trust with the members of your network. And the response to your message, on or offline, depends on the social capital you have created with the network members you are approaching. This is a key component of your personal marketing.

The Simple Truth of Social Capital

Social capital is created wherever positive relationships with others can be found: in the workplace, through networking organizations, while spending time with friends and family, or even on the golf course. You might also generate social capital through your participation in a Linked In group or a private Facebook Page, or by consistently liking and sharing someone's social media posts.

Social capital is the building block of all relationships. Personal marketing, meanwhile, is about creating, managing and *leveraging* your social capital, both on and offline.

Here's an example of what that can look like:

Susan's last book was called Content Marketing Made Easy—Why You Need It, How to Do It.[2] Within a day or two of publication, her publisher called to tell her it had started trending on Amazon. This was great news!

The book was at about #88 in its category. Not bad, considering the number of books available on Amazon With a clear shot at #1 galvanizing her into action, Susan immediately began leveraging her social capital.

There are people out there who run Amazon Best-Seller Campaigns as businesses, and who can a-l-m-o-s-t guarantee that they can get your book to a #1 position on Amazon…for a hefty fee. Instead, Susan called three key members of her network and asked them to support her online inviting people to buy the book.

She then sent out a mass email to her database with the same request, and she shared status updates on all of her social media platforms inviting the people in her online network to purchase the book.

---

[2] https://amzn.to/2Tf7GPp

Then she sat breathlessly in front of her computer and watched. By the time she retired for the night, the book was at #6. She made a few more posts on social media, messaged a few more friends to ask for support, and sent out one more email asking people to buy the book

Then she fell into bed, exhausted but hopeful. When she woke up the next morning, the book had hit #2. The suspense was crackling in the air over a light breakfast, and she posted again to social media.

An hour later, the book crested the charts and settled in at #1. It was thrilling!

Now, aside from being a content marketing consultant, Susan is also a book coach and editor. What do you think the value of a #1 best-selling book on Amazon is to a business professional like her? It's priceless!

And she couldn't have gotten there without the social capital she has created in her online and offline network! This is personal marketing at work. What could it do for you in your business?

PART ONE: EQUIPMENT YOU'LL NEED

Chapter One:

Climbing the Personal Marketing Mountain

Chapter Two:
Referral Marketing to Ease the Incline

Chapter Three:

Content Marketing as Oxygen

Chapter One:

Climbing The Personal Marketing Mountain

Marketing your professional services business is a lot like climbing Mount Everest: success requires vision, preparation, determination and effort. What's more, only those who are driven to reach the pinnacle get to enjoy the thrill of success. And many do not succeed.

Business professionals seeking to create the revenue they truly deserve know all too well how steep their "climbing curve" can be. Only a small percentage can scale those economic heights to enjoy their own personal view of prosperity.

Annual Business Openings with 2013 as Base Year

Year ended	Survivors	Employees	Survival Rate (vs. Year 1)
March 2013	629,078	2,804,566	100.0
March 2014	500,620	2,833,786	79.6
March 2015	433,681	2,870,898	68.9
March 2016	386,033	2,858,300	61.4
March 2017	348,230	2,823,257	55.4

US Bureau of Labor Statistics' Business Employment Dynamics[3]

---

[3] https://www.bls.gov/bdm/us_age_naics_00_table7.txt

21

Here's the quick answer for what percentage of small businesses fail. According to data from the US Bureau of Labor Statistics about 20% fail in their first year, and nearly 50% of small businesses fail in their fifth year.

Why is that? Why do so many businesses, and business professionals, miss their own targets, year after year?

A better question might be: What does it take to win at personal marketing?

The mindset, rituals and habits of the business professionals who win at personal marketing are a lot like those of successful Mount Everest mountaineers.

Consider these statements for both missions:

1. It's a journey. You need to prepare accordingly. Physically. Financially. In every way.

2. You have to work hard to advance every day. Consistency pays.

3. You need to track your progress.

4. You need a compass and a plan.

5. You have to believe in yourself. No Second- guessing, no personal Saboteurs.[4]

6. You have to believe in the mission, and that you will succeed. Passionately.

7. You need a personal support system to maintain your positive attitude.

8. You need to be a lifelong learner.

9. You need to be ready to course-correct.

10. You need a guide. Always.

At the end of this chapter you will find a grid that will invite you to rate yourself on a scale of 1-5 on each of these attributes.

This will allow you to see where you stand with your own Mount Everest, marketing yourself, on and off line.

---

[4] For more on how to overcome the personal saboteurs that might be keeping you from earning the revenue you desire and deserve, read Paula's book, "*Stop The Saboteurs: Conquer Negative Thoughts that Hurt Your Revenue and Your Brand.*" *https://amzn.to/2YHuauN*

Prescription for Success:
Assume That You Are Not Ready for the Journey

The most successful business professionals with whom we have worked *know* that they are not ready for the business climb they are about to make. And they also have a real appreciation for the enormity of the task ahead of them.

They have paid attention to the fact that they require guidance throughout their long journey to success. They are lifelong learners who understand that they will always need to grow, learn, and improve, if they want to survive and thrive.

They also know that they need to "pack" accordingly. Especially, on the financial front. They need to be ready for two years of "no-to-low" revenue, and they need to be prepared to manage the fact that their household will not be enjoying the same largesse as in the past.

They also need to prepare to invest in themselves and their network. If it's Everest we're talking about, you want great equipment—no skimping on the oxygen supply!

If it's marketing your business, you want to be prepared to invest in your physical presence, your networks and your networking events

And you will want to invest in excellent technology, online tools — and perhaps even some outside assistance.

This is a mission that requires support!

This Speaks to the Issue of Mindset

It is said that Walt Disney was fired from his job at a newspaper because he "lacked imagination." He went on to build a business empire based on a highly-creative string of movies, and to which he added theme parks and an endless supply of supporting products.

The first book ever written by now-famous children's writer Dr. Seuss was rejected by 27 different publishers before it finally appeared in print, leading off a publication record that stretched to more than 600 million books sold.

Even famed physicist Albert Einstein started his career with a string of jobs at which he was apparently no raving success.

These people were determined to succeed at any cost!

When one of their efforts rendered the "wrong" results, they used it as information needed to get closer to their goal—rather than as proof they were failures.

Many people who failed generously before succeeding don't look at these experiences as disasters, but rather as character-building exercises that helped them grow. What a great mindset!

Our mindset can support us to the learning of new skills, the completion of difficult tasks and the development of relationships with key people. Or not.

Successful People

Many of the most successful people on the planet were told, at one point in their lives, that they would never amount to anything.

They took those opinions as *information*, rather than as predictions of a foregone conclusion. They chose to become successful in spite of—perhaps even *because of*—the opposition they were facing.

At its most basic, our mindset is a set of thoughts, ideas attitudes and beliefs that determine our outlook on life, our approach to our lives, and, most significant of all, our behavior. In essence, our mindset *drives* our behavior and supports us to the development of habits that affect how we think, feel and act.

It affects how we make sense of the world and how we make sense of ourselves.

It is a key determinant in whether or not an entrepreneur is going to hit his or her goals, or fall far short.

A powerful mindset allows us to learn from our experiences, invest in success and seek assistance when needed. It helps us take a stronger stance with employees, peers and business partners.

It can also support us in setting prices more assertively and steering clear of clients with whom we don`t want to work.

Do You Need to Change Your Idea of What it Takes to Succeed?

Personal marketing represents a paradigm shift for most business professionals who may have spent months or years in a "trial and error" approach to marketing their business.

Personal marketing is not so much something you make time for as it is the centrepoint around which the entire rest of your life revolves. The people who succeed at this game dedicate 20-25 hours a week to their personal marketing activities.

You can actually spend an unlimited amount of time developing relationships with members of your referral network, both on and off line.

And, the more time you spend, the faster you will see positive results.

Plus, it can be fun!

So, the biggest habit you need to cultivate is the lifestyle change that you will have to make in order to strategically devote large chunks of your valuable time to your personal marketing.

Most of us have come to recognize that our habits drive our results: if we are in the habit of putting our keys in the same place when we walk in the door every day, for example, we will always know where they are.

Habits Generate Results

If we are in the habit of brushing our teeth regularly, they will stay healthy longer. And, if we develop habits around carrying out our personal marketing activities, we will generate the results personal marketing can deliver.

Personal marketing is not generally taught in colleges or universities at this time—in fact, even professors of law or business at the graduate level give barely more than a nod to strategic methods of connecting either online or offline.

"Go golfing," is about as good as some of the advice ever gets.

You are more sophisticated than that! Expand your personal marketing bandwidth and get serious about making strategic decisions about how you spend your time. Success takes time! You need to knuckle down and get busy!

Here are some suggestions for moving towards a more powerful personal marketing mindset:

Practice positive self-talk:

Replace:	**With:**
"I can't do it."	"I can't do it *yet*."
"This is impossible."	"This is impossible *unless I change something*."
"I am powerless to change this."	"Maybe I can change one small piece at a time."

Accept new challenges. Our world is changing constantly, and it is unreasonable to expect your business to stay static. Accept that change involves challenge, so you can stop resisting change, and focus on building success.

Do more. Athletes don't simply "think" their way to a gold medal, although here, too, mindset has a powerful role to play. They also train many hours every day *without fail* in order to reach their goals. They do more. Can you decide to do more, too?

Ditch the need for perfection. There is always room for improvement, so while you might never get to "perfect," you can always move on to "better." Just keep looking for improvements.

Celebrate your successes.
You're amazing! Own it!

Don't give up. Look at rejection as misalignment, rather than evidence that you are not "good enough."

If getting good at personal marketing is not your natural inclination, be patient with yourself. It takes time to change habits you've been building your entire life. Change is probably going to feel uncomfortable for a while. That's OK! Everyone who has ever become successful has felt uncomfortable at some stage along the way!

Are you committed to doing this?
If you are, you have come to the right place. *Your Personal Marketing Playbook* (PMP) is designed to make sure that you thrive, not just survive, in the Mount Everest of new business development – both on and offline.

Homework: Your Self-Assessment Grid

On a scale of 1 -5 , 1 = Never, 3 = Sometimes, 5 = Always, please rate your level of readiness to run your business according to each one of these 10 phrases.

(You can also download a version of this assessment at: YourPmp-Hope.com)

WHERE ARE YOU NOW?

Rate your Current Referral System

1 = Never	3 = Sometimes			5 = Always		

Part 1: You

	1	2	3	4	5
I can easily express to others "why I truly enjoy my business."	1	2	3	4	5
I have a clear message about my expertise and deliver it easily.	1	2	3	4	5
I have a clear vision for my business.	1	2	3	4	5

Part 2: Your Target Market

	1	2	3	4	5
	1	2	3	4	5
I can clearly describe my target market.	1	2	3	4	5
I understand what organizations my target market belongs to.	1	2	3	4	5
My networking efforts are focused towards my target market.	1	2	3	4	5
My current clients all reflect my exact target market.	1	2	3	4	5

Part 3: Your People

	1	2	3	4	5
I know who is in my referral network.	1	2	3	4	5
I understand how to move the depth of my relationships.	1	2	3	4	5
I know which network members to deepen relationships with.	1	2	3	4	5

Part 4: Your Activities

	1	2	3	4	5
I strategize proactively to give referrals to my referral network.	1	2	3	4	5
I attend networking events regularly.	1	2	3	4	5
I invest more than 6 hours per week in deepening my relationships.	1	2	3	4	5

Part 5: Equipping Your People

	1	2	3	4	5
I have properly trained my sources how to qualify a referral for me.	1	2	3	4	5
My sources understand what a first appointment with me looks like.	1	2	3	4	5
I have a reward system for my referral sources.	1	2	3	4	5

Part 6: Supporting Your Referral Marketing

	1	2	3	4	5
My social media is planned and strategic.	1	2	3	4	5
My social media campaign also promotes my referral sources.	1	2	3	4	5

Part 7: 2 Overall Referral Marketing Questions

	1	2	3	4	5
I have the time to devote to developing proper referral relationships.	1	2	3	4	5
My business makes good referrals for others.	1	2	3	4	5

Any phrase to which you have responded with a "1", "2" or "3", foretells a challenge ahead that you will need to address now. Wherever you've rated yourself with a clear and confident "4" or "5," you are in a good place, and can lean on this resource in your mindset as you grow your business.

Be careful; make sure that you are being ruthlessly honest with yourself. You might want to discuss your results with your coach. If you don't have one yet, maybe this is a good time to engage one. You can look to him or her to help you stay on track with your business and personal goals. Together, you will set your goals and, as a team, ensure that you reach them.

Once you have completed this grid, and have acknowledged the real challenges at hand, (we like to be honest with you about the perils of your journey), please move on to the next chapter: Referral Marketing to Ease the Incline.

A Definitional Interlude: What is Marketing?

It takes only three-quarters of a second for nearly one billion results to show up in Google in response to the question, "What is Marketing?" Many of those definitions are complicated and, quite frankly, very boring, so we've developed our own definition based on decades of practical experience in the marketing field:

Marketing is the process of starting conversations with the people with whom you want to do business.

You might start those conversations at a networking event or a trade show. You might start those conversations by handing out brochures, business cards, newsletters or key chains. You might also start those conversations through your website, Linked In profile, Twitter feed, or your blog. There are unlimited opportunities out there for starting conversations with people.

But you want to make sure that you put your time, money and energy into starting conversations primarily with people who might want to buy what you are selling.

Marketing Supports the Sales Process

Let's remember that Sales picks up where Marketing ends.

Once you have generated an opportunity for a conversation through your marketing, you are into a sales process that hones in on how that conversation should play out.

When should you follow up? What collateral materials do your referral partners and prospective clients need to help them make a decision? And so on.

If you are focused on generating and leveraging your social capital, the answers to those questions are easier, as your referral relationship will guide you on next steps.

With that in mind, let's look a little more closely at Referral Marketing.

Chapter Two:
Referral Marketing to Ease the Incline

Paula's Story:

Back in the early 2000s, my tennis friends and I would enjoy a post-tennis beer every week after our regular match. It was a great opportunity to stay up-to-date on everyone's lives, and we discussed everything from our children's progress, to troubled marriages, to career and business challenges.

We were there to help one another and, sometimes, to attempt to solve many of the world's problems. (With limited success on that front, although it was a lot of fun trying.) This was long before I became a referral marketing expert, although I had recently started my own business.

One day, I shared with my friends that I was launching a "sales-executive-on-demand" consulting practice.

Unbeknownst to me, the captain of my tennis team was listening very carefully to the details about my new business endeavour.

One day, she asked me to meet with the president of the company at which her husband was an executive and investor. She wanted me to help them with some major sales challenges.

I met with the president, another tennis player from my tennis club, and immediately started a very successful three-year, full-time consulting contract which enriched not only my pocketbook, but also my soul.

The president of the company was kind and thoughtful, and the business—soft laser medical devices—absolutely fascinated me. I learned a lot about the alternative and traditional medical worlds, and I garnered valuable knowledge I did not know I needed. It was a pivotal time in my career.

So, a referral from such an unusual source—the captain of my tennis team—changed my life.

When I learned more about referral marketing, I realized a number of elements had been present in my situation at the time that had actually generated this highly meaningful referral.

We had high trust with one another and we were in a nurturing and positive network at our tennis club. We saw one another frequently, which inspired confidence in each other's businesses, and we shared common values.

It was a veritable recipe for referrals!

Imagine my excitement when I realized that learning about training and coaching business professionals in referral marketing best practices would allow me to intentionally create referrals for my business while helping them grow their businesses exponentially!

My company, Booked Solid, was born, inspired by a referral from the captain of my tennis team. Who knew?

Relationships, and most certainly the strong relationships that create referrals, do not happen overnight, and in most people's worlds, strong relationships do not occur often.

When you combine a trusting relationship with a deep knowledge of your business by a motivated network member, add in your partner's confidence in you, plus knowledge of referral marketing, you will receive very well-qualified, easily-closed, beautiful referrals.

Here's the referral marketing formula:

You + Trust + Deep Knowledge of Your Business + Confidence + Referral Marketing Strategies = Well-Qualified, Easily Closed Referrals

A Definitional Interlude: What is Referral Marketing?

Referral Marketing is the systematic cultivation of business by referral.
In fact, *Referral Marketing* is a system by which business professionals intentionally create, manage and leverage their social capital to generate referrals. Referral Marketing creates a plan to systematically **capitalize** on word-of-mouth support in order to generate referrals.

In fact, referral marketing is the original method of creating new business.
Imagine John the caveman saying to Peter, another caveman, "George, the man who makes spears in our village, is the best around! Go get your weapon from him." John created a referral by sharing his trust in George with Peter. A referral is born. And what is a referral?

A referral is a transfer of trust.

That's right! Referrals cannot happen unless trust is present, which logically leads us to the assertion that trust is the hallmark of both a strong relationship and a good referral.

And never insult a referral by calling it a lead. A lead is an idea, where no trust is transferred. Please do not settle for leads from your network. You want beautiful referrals!

This playbook is dedicated to sharing with you the referral marketing knowledge that you need to create the revenue that you really desire and deserve. *Your* role is to develop those deep business relationships of trust and confidence in you.

You will be completing the personal marketing process when you develop your relationships strategically with both on- and offline strategies.

Let us be clear, however: referral marketing requires an investment here. It is a different sort of investment than any other new business development method you will ever experience.

New Business Development
The good news is that your referral marketing journey will require a much smaller upfront financial investment than any other new business development method. At the same time, the bigger part of your investment will be in time, focus and, yes, **heart**.

Expect a lot of personal growth from your investment in referral marketing. You will cultivate many parts of yourself as you grow your network—your "Stars" or your Referral "A Team"—and the programs of mutual benefit on which you and your team collaborate.

Your referral marketing system is something you build. And the results from these personal investments are going to be exponential. Consider these powerful outcomes from your investment in referral marketing:

1. **The closing rate (the percentage of referred prospects which result in a closed deal) is a whopping 34%!**
   Yes, one in three referrals, where an average amount of trust is transferred, ends up in a deal. But guess what happens to the closing rate when there is a *high* level of trust? It can jump to **80%!** With this level of trust, almost every referral will end up in a close.

   That really high level of trust is created by you and the on-and-offline activities you select for **Your Personal Marketing Playbook (PMP)**.

2. **Your confidence is much higher when you approach a referred prospect.**
   The likelihood of closing an exceptional deal will be higher when you meet a referred prospect *because of your own confidence*. All referred business professionals remark on this feeling. Trust in you has been transferred.

   You already share a respected member of your network with your prospect. You will have your best game on.

Remember to praise your referral source enthusiastically in the meeting with the referred prospect (a key referral marketing strategy).

3. Price is less of an issue with a referred prospect.

Have you ever been in a meeting with a referred prospect when the meeting has gone so well that price becomes less of a concern for the prospect due to the relationship that you have with the referral source? It always amazes me that concern about price can be so quickly diminished by trust that has been transferred.

Trust = Value.
TRUST = $$$.
Very powerful!

4. Adoption of additional services during the first year of business is greater.

There are statistics to support the fact that referred prospects are more open to the addition of more services from a referred vendor within the first year of the business relationship. Interesting...the trust platform from the referral continues to resonate powerfully during the first year. Maybe even until you exit your business...

5. **The Creation of a referral culture within the new relationship pays dividends.**
A referral culture has been modelled by you and your referral source. Even more referrals occur in a relationship that has evolved from a successful referral.

So, reasons for investing in referral marketing abound.

Your investments focus on identifying and building relationships with the people with whom you want to move forward in business, people who will become allies in the ever-important quest to increase revenue.

As you build your relationships with this select group of people, you will be supporting their quest for greater revenue, as well.

A Referral Partnership is a Special Relationship
A referral partnership is the most important business relationship that any business professional can foster. You want to develop these partnerships with people who have **a generous spirit and an approach to the world that is full of abundance.**

After all, it is hoped that you will be living with this choice throughout your business career—and afterwards.

Your referral partner is your "golden goose," always providing you with referrals, as you do the same for them. Your referral partners are special and rare people. Be sure to always take good care of them!

There are eight important considerations to keep in mind as you select the people you want as your Referral Partners:

1. Referral partners are defined as the close members in your network who you like and trust. You know and believe in one another's businesses and you support each other 100%.

2. The relationship has already developed to a stage where you know a lot about what each other offers, and you are raving fans of each other.

3. You share the same target market. Your ideal client is the same as your referral partner's ideal client. This is a key point in a referral partnership. His/her ideal client is the same as yours. You each offer different, and not competitive, services or products.

4. You have both embraced growing your business by referral. Both of you embrace the concept of "Givers Win." You know that if you want to grow your business, you need to give referrals to members of your network. You and your partner have a plan for growing your businesses together.

5. What's more, your referral partners are givers by nature. They understand the law of reciprocity: the more you give, the more you enjoy life and reap its personal and material harvests. They would make good referrals for the people in your network. They want, and can be inspired, to help you.

6. You both have a clear call to action in order that your referral partner can take your prospect to the next step, whether it is a complimentary consulting or coaching session, or an educational seminar.

7. After two-to-three years of focused networking and referral-building, most committed referral marketers have a maximum of four referral partners and more than eight referral sources.

8. You and your referral partner share the same values. You are both givers and believe in the power of growing business by leveraging your network authentically. You both have a unique value proposition to offer your prospects and clients.

Sound exciting? It is! And well worth the networking, qualifying, sharing, communicating, collaborating and other activities that lead to the development of a referral partner.

A Personal Marketing Playbook (PMP) Bonus:

One last key point about integrating referral marketing into your world:

In any organization, especially in a professional services organization, all hands should be on deck to assist with new client development, including, and, especially, the executive levels. How many accountants, lawyers, and consultants ever achieve partner status without bringing new and high-quality clients with them to their lofty new heights?

Not many!

And yet, we have met many business professionals who want to hire a sales professional to handle new business development for them as soon as they can afford them.

The best (and, for some, the worst) news? You, the owner of the social capital, are always the best choice for tapping into that social capital to develop new clients.

You Know What Referral Marketing Is... Now, How Does It Work?

Start by evaluating your strengths and weak-nesses in referral marketing via eight considerations we outlined.

Are you clear on what your values are?

Are you a giver?

Do you know who your target market is?

Do you have a clear call to action?

There's a fair bit of homework to be done before you can start developing and leveraging relationships that qualify as "referral" relationships. This is all crucially important when it comes to taking this all online to address your content marketing efforts, as well, by the way.

The Law of Reciprocity

Positive personal marketing behaviour models a response from members of your network. They want to thank you and respond to the Law of Reciprocity. This Law requires that an act of kindness is always returned by another act of kindness. And so *social capital* is created. Relationships can grow faster if social capital is created by both relationship participants.

How is this done?

By giving, and more giving. And, helping in any way you can, personally and in business.

One-on-one conversations are vitally important: they allow you to find ways to help your prospective referral source or partner.

You can help by connecting them with your friends, or a new supplier, working together on a wedding or a business project or by inviting them to social or business events.

Here's more on how this works:
As you develop your referral marketing acumen, enriched by content/online marketing plays or tactics, your personal network will go through four phases. By the time you have reached the fourth phase, you will have created a referral network for the long term, for as long as you remain in business and beyond. Here are the four phases of a business professional with a network for the long term:

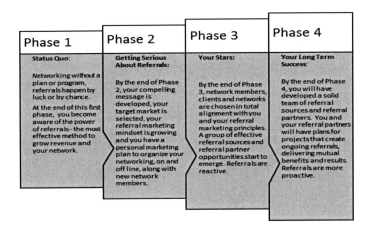

Phase 1	Phase 2	Phase 3	Phase 4
Status Quo:	**Getting Serious About Referrals:**	**Your Stars:**	**Your Long Term Success:**
Networking without a plan or program, referrals happen by luck or by chance. At the end of this first phase, you become aware of the power of referrals - the most effective method to grow revenue and your network.	By the end of Phase 2, your compelling message is developed, your target market is selected, your referral marketing mindset is growing and you have a personal marketing plan to organize your networking, on and off line, along with new network members.	By the end of Phase 3, network members, clients and networks are chosen in total alignment with you and your referral marketing principles. A group of effective referral partner opportunities start to emerge. Referrals are reactive.	By the end of Phase 4, you will have developed a solid team of referral sources and referral partners. You and your referral partners will have plans for projects that create ongoing referrals, delivering mutual benefits and results. Referrals are more proactive.

After years in the referral marketing field, Paula has developed a great checklist for helping you determine where you are on the referral marketing spectrum.

Your answers to the questions in the "Where are You Now?" referral marketing assessment will help give you a great sense of what work remains to be done in order to bring you to a place of referral marketing power.

How did you do? Were you able to identify the areas that need more of your attention?

What is one thing you can do right now to improve your score?

Go ahead — do it now! And keep taking more steps, every day, to align your efforts with the results you want. Success with your personal marketing takes a lot of effort.

Most importantly, it works!

A Definitional Interlude

What is Content Marketing?

Content marketing is about the process of creating a substantial body of content related to your business and the needs of your ideal clients, and sharing it with the people with whom you might want to do business.

The world of content marketing is about becoming a publisher, a creator of content that will support your ideal audience in their drive to live easier lives, in whatever way that might mean to them.

We have wonderful opportunities today to develop and share content through online platforms such as our websites and our Linked In, Facebook, Twitter, Instagram, You Tube, and other channels.

You want your content to position your company and your stories authentically , so they generate trust, credibility and likeability for you, and call upon your viewers and visitors to take another step in a growing relationship with you. In effect, your content represents a massive opportunity to build social capital.

Chapter Three:

Content Marketing as Oxygen

Susan's Story

My team and I have a lot of content on the web sites we maintain for my two businesses. Aside from the standard "Home," "About," "Services" and "Contact" pages, we have a blog that is updated with regular posts, as well as case studies, videos, and free downloadable resource papers.

Most of that information is designed to either provide helpful information or demonstrate what it's like to work with us. Sometimes our content does both.

Aside from all that is our "Contact Us" tab that includes a survey form that people can fill in to describe the topic or project with which they need assistance, and my team and I get an email whenever someone fills this in. The object of the "Work with Us"[5] survey is to generate conversations with people who might become our clients.

---

[5] https://survey.zohopublic.com/zs/myB0Jk

The questions in the survey give us enough information to determine if the individual completing the survey represents a business that might be a good match for what we offer, and their information helps guide the follow-up conversation we book with them.

One beautiful summer day, we received a notification indicating that someone who had filled in the "Contact" form. I was racing out the door to deliver my 16-year-old son to driving school when I saw the notification, and, as soon as I had dropped him off, I checked my phone to read the survey in full.

The project the respondent described was perfect for us! But was there a personal fit between us? We tend to work with our clients for a long time, and my business is a vehicle for adding enjoyment to my life. I want to make sure everyone's goals will be met by a business connection.

Many people feel that internet marketing is impersonal and automatic, cold and unemotional. While it can be, it doesn't have to be. For a professional services provider, it absolutely does get personal!

Remember our definition of marketing earlier in this book? It's the process of starting conversations with the people with whom we want to do business.

While my business does tend to run on referrals, we also get business from our online presence ...but nothing happens until we have that conversation!

Right there in the parking lot of the driving school in my home town, I called the survey respondent and had a wonderful two-hour conversation with one of the most delightful people I have ever met.

A Perfectly-Aligned Project

Not only did this lady have a perfectly-aligned project for us, but she is now a good friend and one of those people who has become a source of referrals for me.

It turned out that she had explored our website fully, looked at a substantial amount of our online content, and she had known immediately that she wanted to exploring working with us.

The conversation was a key part of the confirmation process. And the web content had been the conversation "starter."

Like referral marketing, content marketing gives you an opportunity to personalize your relationships. It serves as another method of creating the kind of social capital that results in interesting revenue by leveraging relationships.

You want to make sure your online content is informational rather than blatantly "sales-y."

As with referral marketing, it's about giving first, and it answers the question:

"What information can I give potential clients and customers that will solve their problems and help them achieve their goals more quickly and effectively?"

Your content has, at its heart, a real respect for potential clients, acknowledging that they might want to conduct considerable research before they engage in a conversation with a potential supplier. It builds trust and authority for you amongst your ideal customers and it also supports your relationship with them.

You Are a Valuable Resource

In providing helpful online content, **you are positioning yourself as a valuable resource** for people who need what you provide.

If you do this well, human visitors and search engines will reward your efforts and you will generate greater revenue as a result.

If you do this as part of your referral marketing strategy, you will also, most importantly, be honouring the people who can bring you referrals and build your business.

Here are some compelling statistics about the success of content marketing from the Content Marketing Institute:[6]

- Content marketing gets three times more leads per dollar spent than paid search

- Content marketing generates more than three times as many leads as outbound marketing, and it costs 62% less

- The number of ads people see on an average day increased from 2,000/day in 1984 to about 5,000/day in 2014, giving rise to a massive use of ad blockers to weed out the noise. Content is rarely, if ever, blocked

- Small businesses with blogs get 126% more lead growth than small businesses without

- 61% of U.S. online consumers have made a purchase after reading product or service recommendations on a blog

- Content marketing has a conversion rate that is six times higher than most other methods of marketing.

- Content creation is the most effective Search Engine Optimization technique

---

[6] http://contentmarketinginstitute.com/2017/10/stats-invest-content-marketing/

There are a host of other surveys out there indicating that a huge amount of business transacted today involves the internet in some fashion.

It all underscores the fact that your content is an opportunity to personalize those trans-actions, to bring a human element into what is otherwise a highly technical arena.

Your online content marketing strategy gives you a bigger online footprint than you, as a small business, might otherwise generate. It should also:

- Support your referral partners

- Allow people to find out more about you

- Help people see what working with you is like

- Confirm the high opinion the members of your referral network have of you

- Show your target audiences who you are and what you can do

- Help educate people about how to improve their own businesses or lives

- Tell people that you and your team are available as experts in your field and

- Increase your credibility

If you do this well, human visitors and search engines will reward your efforts and you will generate greater revenue as a result.

It makes sense that you might want to develop a strong presence online if you want to build your client base.

Other Methods of Online Marketing

There are other methods of online marketing that have a place in a business's marketing matrix, including paid search and pay-per-click campaigns, website development projects that include conversion strategies and conversion architecture, and more.

Without strong content that positions you as the hands-down choice for the businesses and people you are here to serve, however, your other online marketing efforts may not succeed as powerfully as you would like.

And, how else are you going to support your referral partners in large and prominent ways?

Content marketing doesn't replace referral networking; it supports it. You still want face-to-face opportunities to meet people and develop other ways for them to get to know you and what you do.

A Personal Marketing Playbook Bonus:

One last key point about integrating content marketing into your world:

The task of generating and managing your content has to become a high priority in any business today, especially in a professional services organization where personal fit between services provider and client are so key. Your content demonstrates what it might be like to have you on board as a team-mate, and it has a crucial role in search engine optimization (SEO), another important way for people to find out about you and what you do.

In the ever-evolving world of online content, businesses need to consider themselves and their online presence as a publishing centre, as much as an information provider. What kind of content can you provide to support your potential clients or customers?

You Know What Content Marketing Is... Now, How Does It Work?

People might meet you at a networking event, and you may receive terrific referrals from your referral partners... but if anyone is remotely interested in doing business with you, they are going to search you out online.

You want your online content to align with the great things your network is saying about you!

Story telling is an ancient art form and the people who study these things know that ancient humans crouched around campfires together sharing stories of strength and valour, passion and pain long before a printing press (or the internet) was ever a gleaming idea in a questing mind.

The Vehicle of a Good Story

A good storyteller has likely been a necessity in human society since the dawn of time and unlimited wisdom has been passed along painlessly through the vehicle of a good story.

Although the way we tell our stories has changed, their importance is just as significant today as it has always been: people are far more engaged by a good story well told than they are by a simple collection of facts packed together in an orderly row.

As most of us know, life (and business) is anything but consistently orderly and the lyrical surprises inherent in a good story catch our attention like nothing else can, which doesn't mean that the stories you want to tell about your business are epic romances or imaginative swashbucklers.

Your online marketing stories need to be focused on helping your potential customers understand your product or service while lightening their load in some way.

They are an opportunity to support your referral marketing sources and develop deeper relationships with them, and they represent an opportunity to prove that the good things your sources are saying about you are true.

In upping your content game, you are enhancing the reputation of your referral sources because, as we all know, birds of a feather flock together.

How Do You Tell Your Business Stories? Here are some ideas:

- A website that is designed to support all of your personal marketing endeavours

- Regular blog postings

- Downloadable templates or white papers

- A newsletter/email marketing program

- Informational videos

- Free audio recordings

- Case studies about the problems you solve

- Checklists to help people improve a process

- Social media postings

- Linked In activity

- You tube videos

- SlideShare presentations and

- Podcasts

It's important that you post new content to your online "real estate" consistently. A blog that is updated every six or eight months will add little value to your online reputation whereas one that is refreshed once a week will pack a much more powerful punch.

Your content needs to appeal to two separate audiences: the real people who might potentially buy from you and the web crawlers that want to know if you merit a Page One search ranking. That means your content needs to be cleverly written and optimized for search.

What Problems Do You Solve, And for Whom?

Content marketing is about *creating* a substantial body of content related to your business and the needs of your ideal clients and *sharing* it through online platforms such as your website and your Linked In, Facebook, Twitter, You Tube, Instagram and other profiles.

You want the content to tell your company story authentically so that it generates trust, credibility and likeability for you, and calls upon your viewers and visitors to take another step in a growing relationship with you.

For example:

- A business that doesn't want to ask customers for testimonials because they are concerned about safeguarding customer privacy can create a blog post about how focused they are on their customers' confidentiality. OR they can ask a referral partner to write a guest blog that includes a comment that supports their reputation for excellence

- A business that has been around for 30 years can create an interesting article about how their industry has changed over the past few decades (and how they have changed with it)

- You could develop case studies about the work you do – ask your referral partners to be interviewed for great comments about you, and return the favour!

- Every case study can be turned into a power point presentation that can be posted to the web as a SlideShare presentation

- SlideShare presentations can be turned into videos

- You can create high-quality videos in which your referral partners are filmed saying great things about you...and do the same for them!

- Every time you post content to your website or other online platform you can tweet about it or create a status update sending people to the content so they can find out more

- Share status updates that say great things about your referral partners

- And remember that all of this content signals to the search engines that there is something good going on at your place of business, so they will reward you with better rankings

More and better content will help you shine online. Your content helps drive your online rankings, and the more organized and effective you are in developing your content, the more people know about you, and the more you can grow your audience.

Try This Just for Fun:

Do an online search for you or your business. Next, search out a competitor. Now, answer these questions:

- Are there more references to your competitor on the Search Engine Results Pages (SERPs)?

- Are those references posted on quality websites?

- Can you find lots of links to their website?

- Are your ideal customers more likely to find a reference to you or your competitor online?

- What can you learn about the opportunities for developing content—and the social connection it invites—through your competitor's content?

Red Bull Has This Figured Out

Red Bull is an energy drink company that runs the Red Bull Content Pool. It stocks more than 50,000 photos and 5,000 videos about sports, culture and lifestyle. The company makes the material available to their 4.8 million subscribers, which tend to be TV stations, platform providers and cinema distributors.

The content they provide does not proclaim the benefits of drinking Red Bull, the beverage. But it says a lot about Red Bull as an adjunct to a lifestyle. You can check this out at: redbullcontentpool.com/content/international

Another example: Campbell Soup Company provides excellent food-related information on its website, including great recipes, and information about the ingredients in the food it produces: campbellsoupcompany.com/.

And HubSpot, a digital marketing company, provides plenty of terrific information about how to implement best practices in your online marketing: hubspot.com/.

You Still Need to Talk to Real People!

Even if you create a terrific pool of practical content, you still have to talk to people, and your own process of making a sale still stands.

However, your content marketing efforts will give your prospects more opportunities to get to know more about your company and what you can do for them. Now, take a look at the following questionnaire and see how your online content stacks up. Is there room for improvement? What does that look like?

Action You Can Take Today		
Take an Inventory of Your Existing Web Content. Do You Have:		
	Yes	No
A website that is less than three years old		
A blog that you update regularly		
A company newsletter that you send out regularly		
A social media presence (Twitter, Facebook, Linked In, Google+)		
Five or more professionally produced videos		
A press outreach program		
Five or more case studies on your website		
Five or more articles about your products or services		
A white paper that prospective customers can download		
A desire to improve your online presence		

You can download a version of the checklist from Susan's site at: YourPmp-Crossman.com.

Your Score: 10 checks = You've got this!
5-10 checks =You have some work to do
3-5 checks = Time to develop a strategy around this? Less than 3 checks =It's not too late!
What one thing can you do NOW to change your score and generate better results online?

Chapter Four:
Your Personal Marketing Playbook:
Focusing on your Destination

If it's to be, It's up to me!
William H. Johnsen

As you have learned from the first few chapters of *Your Personal Marketing Playbook (PMP)*, there is much to consider, and do, when creating a business, if you want to put yourself onto a solid footing for success.

As we've noted, Personal Marketing is a combination of two new business development methods used by professional service providers to create and leverage a dedicated network that results in ongoing and high-quality referrals for easily-closed business.

These successful outcomes are generated through informed and targeted personal activities (referral marketing) and a strategic and active online presence providing ongoing value (online content marketing).

Both methods require authentic and personal involvement, making our definition of the term "Personal Marketing" an effective term for this highly productive, unique, and evolving method of new business development.

67

Referral Marketing + Content Marketing = Personal Marketing

One of the key reasons 20% of businesses fail in their first year and 50% by their fifth year is that business owners don't always fully appreciate the task at hand.

Just think of the problems you would generate for yourself if you turned up at Mount Everest Base Camp in cotton shorts and chic leather sandals!

You would be woefully underprepared for such a complex and demanding adventure. (Fortunately, for Mount Everest novices, there is now a thorough vetting process.)

For you, the budding business owner, and professional service provider, however, the vetting process is built upon a combination of your revenue (or lack thereof), and your diminishing bank balance.

Not to mention, your life partner and family members who are less-than-happy when the revenue doesn't mount up as planned. You might not be in business after your first two years.

WE DON'T WANT THAT TO HAPPEN!

If you're thinking that Personal Marking methods seem to require a lot of time, work and discipline, you would be right!

It *does* take a lot of time to employ Personal Marketing methods. If you are executing properly on these methods, and, if you include travel time to events and 1:1 meetings, plus daily time to keep in touch with your network online, plus creating content for online platforms, you should be budgeting 20 -25 hours a week for new client development. *At least!* Every week.

One study of time invested vs. referral results looked at the behaviour of 12,000 business professionals. It found that people who invested 20+ hours a week in relationship-building and strategic activities received 70% of their business by referral.[7]

Business Networking and Sex, It's Not What You Think by BNI founder Dr. Ivan Misner, found that people who invested the average number of hours that most business professionals invest in their networking—that is, 6.1 hours per week for women and 6.3 hours for men—received only 10% of their business through referrals.

---

[7] https://www.amazon.com/Business-Networking-Sex-What-Think/dp/1599184249/ref=tmm_pap_title_0?_encoding=UTF8&qid=&sr=

The same study noted that 90% of business professionals say their business comes from "networking." So, it stands to reason that business professionals, who are not "out there" networking, on and off line, are not going to see the results for which they are hoping.

New Business Development
Therein lies the real issue why business professionals fail to succeed with their businesses or practices. They are not committed or, more often, do not know they need to be committed, to at least 20-25 hours of new business development activities per week. And they end up with very disappointing, life-changing (not in a good way) results.

If you follow the activity outline we've provided later in this book, it is likely that you will be up and running smoothly after your first two years.

If you are not committing to, and executing on, 20-25 hours of referral and content marketing activities (i.e. personal marketing activities) for your first two years of business, your ability to stay in business will be anyone's guess.

The question is: "Are you willing to leave your business to luck and happenstance"?

Would you prepare for a Mount Everest climb in cotton shorts and flimsy footwear? Our guess is that you picked up this book precisely because your answer is a full-on, "*NO!*"

Let's roll up our sleeves and review the pieces that you must have in place before you can start your daily playbook activities.

Armed with a powerful, fully-optimized network integrated with an equally impactful online presence, there is a far greater likelihood that you will reach your business summit and create the revenue that you desire and deserve. It is our intention that you will thrive with your professional service business for a long time.

How will you achieve this lofty goal?

By following our step-by-step plan for all of your new business development activities — both on and off line.

We're cheering you on from the sidelines!

Digging Into Your Inner Wisdom

The key is to make it your own, and we invite you to dig deep into your inner wisdom and build your plan. In the next chapter, we introduce you to a Planning Ladder model, which will provide you with the structure you will need to start your Personal Marketing Playbook Plan (PMPP).

Your Personal Marketing Playbook

PART TWO: YOUR MAP TO SUCCESS

Chapter Five:
The Planning Ladder—Passion, Vision, and Mission

Chapter Six:

An Important Detour Into Branding-Land

Chapter Seven:

Goals

Chapter Eight:

Strategies, Actions, Problems, Drama

Chapter Five:

The Planning Ladder - Passion, Vision, and Mission

The Big Picture and The Planning Ladder

As we noted earlier, a lot of businesses, like a lot of marriages, don't end up making it for the long haul.

There are many reasons behind this dramatically high failure rate, but they usually lead back to one main culprit: the failure to create "The Big Picture" for the business. This is no less true in marriages.

Statistics show that couples whose marriages fail have not had the crucial ongoing conversations about "Big Picture" issues like values and approaches to parenting, topics around which understanding and alignment will ensure the healthy development of their marriage.

In business, entrepreneurs do not have enough critical conversations with themselves, and their business, about the "Big Picture" topics like their alignment with their business, their monetary goals, and their exit strategy.

While we cannot help you with marriage advice, we will point you in the right direction about "The Big Picture" conversations you need to have about your business.

To assist with this task, we have brought in the Planning Ladder. It neatly outlines the topics for which you need clear answers before moving forward with any business actions, on or off line.

In a hectic "bricks and clicks" world, it is so easy to become caught up in the actions of promoting your business without engaging in the higher order of the "Planning Ladder."

The Planning Ladder covers eight areas:

Passion
Vision
Mission
Goals
Strategies
Actions
Problems
Drama

With the Planning Ladder, you will note that "Actions" happen only once you have fulfilled the five other areas that require focus and alignment of your personal and business aspirations and goals. We know it might be tempting to ignore these steps.

Chunking your brilliant idea for a business down into the kind of detail the Planning Ladder requires might seem like a tedious prospect, but it is an investment that will pay enormous dividends in both the online and offline worlds!

Let's break each one of the eight elements of the Planning Ladder down into bite-sized pieces and get set up for creating your Personal Marketing Playbook Plan.

THE PLANNING LADDER

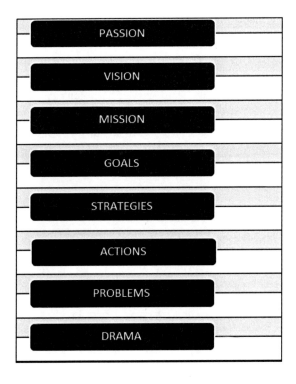

PASSION – Starting with Your Why

A PMPP Must Do:

Make sure your passion and your business are precisely aligned and articulated

Passion, once such a forbidden topic, has become an important word in the business dictionary.

This word, banned in the Victorian era, is now being used on Canadian milk cartons brought to us by a major supplier of dairy foods, Saputo. "Our New Look Reflects Our Passion" is the proud proclamation used in the announcement of the company's packaging upgrade—demonstrating how far we have progressed with the recognition of this critical word in life and business.

Bankers, accountants, alternative providers of business funding, lawyers, consultants, speakers, and, most certainly, coaches, understand that all successful business owners must have passion for their business.

The passion usually comes from a deep desire to solve the problem around which the business's products or services have been developed.

'Sometimes, however, the requisite passion for the business may come from the business owner's burning drive for independence, massive success, fulfillment of a family legacy, or a combination of all three.

Whatever the reason, and there is always a deep-seated reason to uncover, the business owner must find his or her passion, package it appropriately using the Planning Ladder concepts, and share the story of their passion, whenever they can.

Start with Why

This is the all-important "Why" that Simon Sinek writes about in his well-known book entitled, *Start With Why*[8]. His Ted Talk at: ted.com/talks/simon_sinek_how_great_leaders_i nspire_action also speaks to the importance of connecting, and articulating, your "why."

Think of it this way: are you going to be more engaged with a business owner who really cares about the service or product that they provide, or with a person who is merely going through the motions?

---

[8] www.startwithwhy.com

Paula's Passion Story:

At the end of my third-grade year, the education powers-that-be decided to "skip" me and nine of my peers into Grade Five. That fall, we were all thrust into Grade 5, with children who were a year or two older than us.

It was terrifying!

The long-term results of this treatment of bright and scholarship-track students were that only two out of the 10 of us completed high school. Young lives were ruined, traumatized by ill-conceived notions of managing capable kids.

My passion is based on the commitment that I never want to see anyone short-changed from the education they need in order to reach their true level of greatness.

Client Development Training

I see the same gap experienced by myself and my fellow "skippees" in the world of business professionals. These folks require client development training and coaching as much as they require technical training for the delivery of their professional services.

They need this client development coaching and training in order to succeed and move up the ladder to become a partner in their firms, or create the revenue that they deserve for their practice.

Susan's Passion Story:

When I was a little girl I used to climb up into the welcoming arms of the apple tree in my back yard and spend hours daydreaming, writing and imagining.

I could be anything I wanted in the safety of that non-judgmental haven, and I could dream any dream my young heart could conjure.

As I became older, and became ever more committed to the life of a writer, I realized that the world was not as comfortable a place for dreamers as I wanted it to be.

Bridging to the Future

My passion is based on my commitment to helping anyone who has ever felt like an outsider in the online "playground" understand that they are actually a bridge to their own, and someone else's, "happily ever after."

There are some wonderful businesses and business professionals active online today who have powerful and valuable solutions to other people's problems.

Unfortunately, they either don't know what they're doing with their online properties, or lack the skill set to express their value proposition in elegant and compelling ways.

I am determined to help those people feel safe and welcome, and to help them tell their business stories in ways that resonate with the people they are here to serve.

Don't be surprised about what you learn about yourself when your business is plugged into the passion of your being.

To quote a line from the movie, *Flashdance*, **"Find your passion – and make it happen!"** Your tribe will be able to pick up your authenticity a mile away. On or off line!

Coaching Note:

Ask your coach to help you connect your heart with the business you have chosen to create.

VISION

A PMPP Must Do: Make sure that you articulate your vision for your business.

The next step in your progress along the planning ladder is to articulate your Vision. It is imperative for successful Personal Marketing that you articulate it and share, share, share.

Keep your core values close at all times. Here are some visions from notable businesses today:

IKEA: "To create a better everyday life for many people"

Wimbledon: "In pursuit of greatness"

Life is Good: "To spread the power of optimism"

Your vision of your company or practice declares what your business will look like in five, 10 or 15 years, reflecting the values by which you want to live and work. Your vision statement brings your "why" and "how" together to inform your audience about what they can expect to see from your business.

As you will note from the above examples, the more inspiring the vision that you share with your clients, referral sources network members, and online community, the more likely that vison will be embraced and shared, so it can inspire others.

As your business or practice grows, your objectives and goals will change.

As your goals are met, you need to revise your vision statement to reflect the new levels of greatness to which you are aspiring.

The Absence of a Vision

In fact, the absence of a vision is a big challenge for professional service providers, and many folks living unfulfilling lives. When asked to measure where they are against where they want to be, many unfulfilled people are at a loss to describe where they want to be. A conversation from the book *Alice in Wonderland* comes to mind, as it reflects where most of us have been at some point in our lives:

> *"Cheshire Puss," she began, rather timidly, as she did not at all know whether it would like the name: however, it only grinned a little wider.*
>
> *'… she went on. "Would you tell me, please, which way I ought to go from here?"*
>
> *"That depends a good deal on where you want to get to," said the Cat.*
>
> *"I don't much care where—" said Alice.*
>
> *"Then it doesn't matter which way you go," said the Cat.*
>
> *"—so long as I get SOMEWHERE," Alice added as an explanation.*
>
> *"Oh, you're sure to do that," said the Cat, "if you only walk long enough."*
>
> - **Lewis Carroll**, *Alice in Wonderland*

"Getting somewhere" in business is not inspiring to any one, especially not to the originator of such a lacklustre statement.

Thus, creating a vision is at the top of the Planning Ladder order, second only to Passion. It should inspire you, the business owner, your clients, prospects, members of your network and all of those who will come to appreciate you.

Here are our Vision Statements to help you with ideas for your own:

Susan's Vision Statement:

To support peace and prosperity through excellence in communication

Paula's Vision Statement:

To always create Abundance.

What is the big picture for your business? In fact, what is *your* big picture? Your life purpose? What were you set on this world to do? Be sure to answer this question to become clear on what vision you would like to fulfill for yourself and your business. Your happiness depends on your answer.

Coaching Note:

Ask your coach to help you articulate your vision.

MISSION

A PMPP Must-Do: Define your mission statement. Answer the Five Big Questions that Your Network Needs to Know about You. Get Clear about Your Brand.

The Mission section of your plan encompasses the key components of your Personal Marketing Playbook. You are answering all of the five questions that your network and potential audience members need to know about you:

1. What do you do?

2. Who do you serve?

3. What are your products and services?

4. What is unique about you?

5. Why do you do what you do?

The importance of a mission statement for corporations has been well-publicized. What has *not* been as well-appreciated and promoted is the importance of mission statements for business professionals and small businesses. We will remedy this situation with the formula we are about to share here.

The mission statement defines the "what" and "who" of a business as opposed to the "why" and "how," which are to be found in the Passion and Vision statements. The formula that encapsulates the requirements of a mission statement, with a PMP touch, is as follows:

- Ensure that you use simple language with a message that is repeatable and short
- Create a big goal for your business
- Address a specific problem

Here is a left brain (logical, process-driven) structure to help guide you through the process:

I/We provide _____

(3-4 word descriptor of products and services)

to _____

(target market descriptor)

in order that they _____

(emotional benefit of working with your/company/organization).

Here are examples of three well-crafted mission statements to help give you context and ideas for your mission statement:

1. *"We strive to be the global leader in the sporting goods industry with brands built on a passion for sports and a sporting lifestyle!"* —Adidas

2.   *"We seek to be Earth's most customer-centric company for four primary customer sets: consumers, sellers, enterprises, and content creators."* - Amazon

3.   *"To refresh the world; to inspire moments of optimism and happiness; to create value and make a difference."* - Coca Cola

In the Personal Marketing world, corporate mission statements look a lot like your answer to the "What do you do?" question that you will want to prepare before attending any more networking events.

Crafting a powerful answer to the seemingly simple question of "What do you do" marks the beginning of taking control of your networking and referral-building destiny.

Your network will need a clear, benefit-driven, memorable, and highly repeatable statement that they can share readily with any member of their network.

Paula's Mission Statement:

Left Brain Structure (logical, process-oriented):
I help delighted business professionals be booked solid by referral.
Right Brain Structure (creative, connecting):
To create abundance for business professionals.

Susan's Mission Statement:

Left Brain Structure (logical, process-oriented):
I provide content-related support to business professionals and firms that are using their skills and talents to make the world a better place.
Right Brain Structure (creative, connecting):
To create peace and prosperity for business professionals and their communities.

Coaching Note:

Ask your coach to help you with your Mission Statement and your "What do you do?" answer. Be sure to THINK BIG.

Your coach will help you to find the answers to the "what" and "who" questions that are key to your success. And, by the way, the question of "Who do you serve?" is important for your business, as it defines your target market.

The "What" is about the products and services that you will provide to meet their need.

"Who do you serve?" leads right into the question of how you are going to brand yourself. What will your company name, logo, website, LinkedIn profile, and business card say about your business? It's time to talk brand.

More on "What Do You Do?"

What is it about your business that will intrigue people and motivate them to take another step in a business relationship with you? We've talked about this earlier in the book, and hopefully you completed the exercises around it!

Remember, there are five questions for which all of your network members require strong, clear answers before they are comfortable providing you with a referral. And you want to answer these questions in a single, powerful sentence.

What do you do?
Who do you serve?
What are your products and services?
What is unique about you?
Why do you do what you do?

Here are some examples:

Paula's Response to "What Do You Do?
I help talented business professionals become happily booked solid with referrals.

Susan's Response to "What Do You Do?"
I help established businesses add value to the world through outstanding online content.

Putting it All Together

If you still don't know what your answer to this question is, then spend some time filling in these blanks:

"I help _____

(your ideal client)

_____

(create/generate/support/resolve/develop)

_____."

(the results you deliver or the emotional state your ideal client will have after working with you)

I Want People to _____.

(The Action you want people to take)

Chapter Six:
An Important Detour Into BrandingLand

Before going any further down the Planning Ladder, let's take a peek at "Branding." Your brand will have everything to do with your success and you will find that you refine it as your business matures.

Looking Out for Your Brand

Centuries ago, the word "brand" meant to permanently mark something, usually an animal, with a hot iron. It denoted ownership. Everyone had their own unique visual mark so that their possessions were instantly identifiable. There could be no mistaking someone's cows when they were found wandering through a field somewhere. The brand was clear to all who saw it.

Today, a lot of people tend to think that a brand is pretty much code for a logo. With such a compelling history, this is, of course, forgivable. But a brand is so much more than that. It's about what that logo represents.

Let's take a deeper look.

Personal marketing, being a type of marketing, includes an understanding of branding. When it's done properly, a branding research project is conducted over a number of months and results in a massive document that is full of key information about your company, your ideal customers, your competitors and your opportunities.

It results in information that will help you get the most out of your marketing communication dollars.

The Key True Messages

A branding exercise will stray into the ever-important area of your logo, as well as the key true messages your ideal clients or customers need to hear about your business in order to know that you are the ideal supplier for them. It conveys emotion and personality.

And, in an ideal world, the actions you take with the members of your network, and the content you create, all follow your branding.

Many branding experts note that your brand represents the promise you make to your customer about what they can expect from your products and services. It differentiates your business from those of your competitors, and it expresses who you are, who you want to be and who people perceive you to be.

94

Are you the innovator in your industry?

The creative problem-solver?

The high-cost, high-quality option, or the low-cost, get-the-job-done alternative?

You can't be all things to all people and your brand represents the start of a relationship with the people with whom you want to do business. Your website, packaging and promotional materials—into all of which your logo should be integrated—communicate your brand.

Birds of a Feather

As we noted earlier "birds of a feather flock together." The set of expectations people develop about you and your business will be partly based on their assessment of the people whose company you keep.

That's partly why referrals can be so powerful: a good referral from a person of high integrity is worth its weight in gold!

If you haven't investigated your brand yet, and you haven't formalized the information you've accumulated about it in a document that anyone can read, the people who create content for you are going to have to guess about what your target customers need to know about you in order to find you appealing.

What's more, being clear about your values, mission and purpose will help you determine who is in alignment with them and, therefore, will help you figure out who belongs in your referral network.

The Importance of Brand Messaging
As much as possible, you want your referral partners' brand messaging to be a nice fit with your own.

By the way, your ideal client is not "Everybody." A copywriter can't write to appeal to an "everybody." But they CAN write to appeal to the 47-year-old Chief Financial Officer of a company that is growing like gangbusters and struggling with cash flow.

As the owner of a small business, where every dollar counts, you have to start conversations that might lead to a sale with the people who are likely to buy what you're selling.

"Everybody" doesn't need what you offer. But your ideal customer is eagerly scanning the horizon of their world hoping you will show up in it someday.

THOSE are the people your personal marketing should be targeting, so you need to maximize your chances of finding them.

What Goes into Getting Clear on Your Brand?

It does take some time and effort to do this work, and whether you plan to coordinate it all internally, or hire someone else to do the leg work for you, it's probably helpful to get guidance from a branding expert, or hire a coach, to help you gain clarity.

These people know the questions to ask, and branding experts, in particular, are quite often experts in graphic design, which is a key element of your brand expression.

The assistance will be helpful because your brand requires you to get clear on:

- Your ideal customer

- Your company's values

- Your company's "personality"

- Your vision for your company

- The issues that differentiate your company from your competition

- The main benefits of your products or services

- The ways in which your business is better than other companies

- The ways in which other companies are better than yours

- The things other companies are doing that you could do be doing, too –
with your own "twist"

- The areas of excellence that you don't tell people about

- Your customer's values

- The products or service areas you want to expand

- The products or service areas you should consider dropping

- The products or services your customers love

- The products or services your customers don't care about

- The aspects of your business that your customers love

- The aspects of your business that your customers wish you would improve

- What you could do to improve your marketing

- The visual imagery that is likely to appeal to your ideal customers

Whew! That's an exhausting list, isn't it? The point of acquiring all that information is so you can package it up into marketing materials— your logo, your website, your brochures, your online content and anything your company produces to speak for it—in a way that will immediately appeal to your ideal customers.

What's more, having referral partners who share the same ideal audience as you will save a lot of time and effort in your marketing: one good referral will take you on a shortcut straight to your decision-maker's office door!

Your Target Audience in Detail:
Some branding experts want to know details about your ideal customer that might even include the kind of toothpaste they use (yes, there are times when that could be important!). But, generally speaking, here is what will be helpful to know:

- **Demographics**
  The people who are creating content (or logos or websites) on your behalf need to know as much as possible about your target audience.

Specifically, you want to know their:
- o Age
- o Gender
- o Education
- o Occupation
- o Income Level
- o Status: married, single, widowed, childless, etc.

- **Geographic and Lifestyle Factors**
  How do the people you are trying to attract live – and where?
  - o Are they rural and have to drive everywhere?
  - o Or do they live in cities and take transit to work?
  - o What kind of weather is typical for the area?
  - o Are they spenders, or are they conservative with their money?

- **Customer Needs**
  What does your ideal customer need? What pain are they in, and why? For example, is training important to them? Or regulatory compliance?

- **Behaviours**
  Look at your customers' behaviour over the past few years. Can you see any trends? Do they sacrifice quality for price in some areas, or vice versa?

- **Psychographic Details**

  Are there any personal traits typical to your ideal customer? Are they early risers? Fans of one sport over another? Do they favour Android, Blackberry or iPhone? Do they get their news on TV or via the internet? Outlook or Gmail?

Once you've found answers to all of this information, you can start to put together a detailed profile of your ideal customer. In marketing-speak, we call this a "Persona." Some marketers call them your "Avatar."

Developing Your Personas

You may have different personas for the various products or services that your business offers. Give them each a name, a code word that represents all of the people who might possibly want what specific sets of products or services that you are selling.

And keep that persona in mind every time you develop online content for your business or consider attending a networking event.

Just like in days of yore, you want your brand to help people instantly recognize your business – so that you can stand out in any field.

Here's Susan's Marketing Avatar:

I would like to introduce you to Jane, Our Ideal Content Marketing Client

Demographics:

- She is a middle-aged professional, in a committed relationship living in a large North American city
- She earns a comfortable living from a professional services business that she has built from scratch
- She has two children who are finished their education and who have left home
- She is university-educated, and has a degree in Life
- Since graduating from university, she has had a number of jobs but has been working in his/her current business for at least 10 years

Day-to-Day

- A typical day starts around 6:00 am with a cup of good coffee, a run-down of the headlines and a review of any emails that have come in overnight
- Home is a comfortable residence in a nice neighbourhood; she and her

husband have an aging dog, Hank, who has been with the family for 12 years
- Jane drives a Cadillac CTS
- My ideal client and her partner take two good holidays every year – once in the early spring and once in late fall
- Fun is about getting together with friends for a barbecue, seeing the kids when they come home, dining out, taking hikes
- She is intense about work but has a good sense of humour. She is open to conversations about human nature, personal transformation and spirituality, and she will go to church on occasion.

Pain

- Jane has worked hard for years to build her company. It's been tough, but success is coming. The business provides a service that makes the world a better place *somehow*. Now Jane wants to double earnings, but she isn't sure how to go about it. She knows it involves marketing, an area s/he hasn't invested a lot of time and energy into developing.

- The pain, therefore, is that Jane needs to "get some marketing" but she doesn't understand how this new world of online marketing works – it is very confusing

- She doesn't know how to go about hiring someone to do the marketing on his/her behalf, or how to assess if the person offering marketing services is going to do a good job. But she does trust her instincts.
- She knows she has to start soon – in fact this should have been on the radar a year or more ago—but life is busy, and this is overwhelming

Goals

- Set up a content marketing program that will tell the company's story to the people who need what s/he's selling
- Improve the company's search engine rankings
- Reach a wider audience
- Generate more revenue

Other

- The company website was set up by a friend's cousin about seven years ago.
- She has a profile on Linked In. For some reason.
- She thinks Twitter and Facebook are silly
- There are some business videos up on YouTube that were shot in order to highlight the business

Because I "know" Jane well, I keep her in mind when I write something for my business. I have given this information to the graphic designer who creates visual content for my business (including the new website I've developed), and anyone else who might create marketing materials for us.

I don't have to have a long conversation with anyone I hire to service my business – I just hand them my persona details and they know immediately who I would like to have conversations with about the services my business provides. It is so simple. I like simple.

Here's Paula's Marketing Avatar:

I would like to introduce you to Peter/ Francesca, My Ideal Referral Marketing Client

Demographics:

- S/He is a 55-year-old person living in a large North American city
- S/He earns their living from a professional service business that they have built from scratch, receiving referrals from their current, underdeveloped network
- S/He has two children who are finished their education and who have left home

- S/He is university-educated, and likely has a professional designation as an accountant, lawyer, engineer, architect or is a consultant in a specialized area
- Since graduating from university, s/he has worked in a corporate environment and decided a few years ago that they would like to open their own practice

Day-to-Day

- A typical day starts around 7:00 am with a cup of good coffee/herbal tea, a run-down of the headlines and a review of any emails that have come in overnight
- Home is a comfortable residence in a nice neighbourhood that Peter/Francesca shares with a spouse (who works in education) and a dog, Vivid, who has been with them for 12 years
- They have two vehicles— an Audi A 4 that Peter/Francesca drives to work and a Jeep for weekends and road trips. They have a cottage in the Blue Mountains.
- They and their family take two good holidays every year – once in the early spring and once in late fall
- Fun is about getting together with friends for a barbecue or poker night, seeing the kids when they come home, meals out, watching hockey, golf and tennis

- Peter/Francesca are intense about their work but have a good sense of humour. They have various hobbies and are active members of their community.
- They are well-known for their work in local charities. They are lifelong learners and are likely to be news hounds. They have a spiritual interest and appreciate the power of alignment between their personal life and their work.

Pain

- Peter/Francesca have developed a practice that has fed their family for a number of years. At the same time, they know that they could do a lot more business, maybe double what they are doing now. They often think about what they would do with all that extra money. Peter/Francesca feel that they are not doing the "right things" to grow their business but they don't know what those activities might be. They feel alone in their pool of ignorance.
- Their pain is that they want to grow their business by referrals, they might even know that they have created a good network.
- At the same time, Peter/Francesca have no idea how to grow and leverage their network for referrals and opportunities.

- Peter/Francesca want to do something about their situation now but they don't know what that solution might be.
- They are frustrated and disappointed with themselves because they know that they could do so much better. They know that they do important work and could help so many more people.
- Peter/Francesca want some help – but who should S/He trust?

Goals

- Create a referral marketing plan that grows and leverages Peter/Francesca's network
- Develop a "referral mindset" that ensures well-qualified referrals continue to flow into their practice for the rest of its life
- Develop an accountability system with a partner who will be there to support them and their business efforts
- Create the revenue Peter/Francesca desires and deserves

Other

- Peter/Francesca have a "ho-hum" business card and website
- They don't know how to describe their business very well and are not sure if what they are saying is serving their practice very well

- Peter/Francesca has a profile on Linked In. Same (or different) message as their business card and website. It's not really working either.

The most interesting part about developing your avatar is that they begin to look a lot like you.

That's a very good "thing." People buy from people who are like themselves.

You will be attracting clients who share your values and will appreciate the expertise that you bring to their world.

Referral marketing at its finest is when you are delighted by the company of your own clients.

How About You? Who is Your Ideal Client?

Next Steps on the Ideal Client Front

Now that you know who your ideal clients are, and what challenges them, think about who your referral sources and partners are, and what kind of referrals they seek.
The more clarity you have around these two questions, the more effective you can be in your personal marketing.

Your Personal Marketing Playbook

We mentioned earlier that the best marketing creates a highly targeted campaign for an ideal client, that is, a specific individual with specific problems and needs.

You want to build your business relationships—both on-and-offline—around those people, and make it clear to everyone you meet who you are, who you serve and how you help.

What pain is your ideal client experiencing that you can alleviate or eliminate? And what specific results can you deliver that will take them out of their pain?

What relief do they yearn for in their businesses (or in their lives, if you are a B-to-C business) that you can help deliver? The answers to those questions are key.

Your referral sources and partners will be grateful for all of this information and for any tools that you can provide them, such as solid marketing information and powerful case studies.

They can share this knowledge with their networks. And create referrals for you.

So, let's do this together.

This may seem repetitive, but we now want you to go a little deeper with your thinking.

110

Answer the following question now to gain more clarity on this issue:

My ideal client struggles with:

_____

_____

_____

_____

_____

Got that? Good! Now let's move on to the next step: setting some goals.

Action You Can Take Today:

Build the persona that represents your ideal customers. Include information that includes that person's:

Demographics
Geographic and Lifestyle Factors
Their needs and the pain they are in that you are uniquely suited to solving
Purchasing or other Behaviours
Psychographic Details

Chapter Seven:
Goals

We have defined the top three rungs of the PMP Planning Ladder: Passion, Vision and Mission. And we have talked about all of the preparation that you need to create a really solid brand that will serve you and your business. Let's climb to the fourth rung, "Goals," where Passion, Vision and Mission start to translate into action and we become aware of "The Power of Goals."

GOALS
A PMPP Must-Do: Set goals. Stay accountable to your goals every day.

People with clear, written goals, accomplish far more in a shorter period of time than people without them could ever imagine.
Brian Tracy

Almost every motivational guru on the planet will confirm that if you want to succeed in any area, you need to identify your goals and write them down.

It's the first step towards turning something that is invisible—an idea of what you would like in your life—into something that is visible—the concrete manifestation of your desire.

There are a number of powerful reasons for setting goals. The process helps you:

- Assert more control over your life

- Eliminate distractions

- Decide how to most profitably spend your time and money

- Be more accountable for your actions

- Feel more motivated

- Focus your energy on what *you* desire, rather than on what other people want you to have, be or do

- Move out of your comfort zone and into a state of greater fulfillment

- Live a better life

What is a Goal?
At its most basic, a goal is an end toward which effort is directed.

In terms of your personal marketing, you might set a specific annual revenue goal that can be further broken down into a specific number of dollars generated per month.

Some people go deeper into their numbers to determine how many sales conversations they need to have every month in order to meet their revenue goals.

Conversion Rates

For example, at the moment, without the benefit of referral marketing strategies, you might know that you generally convert one out of every "X" sales leads into a client, and one client is worth, say $3,000 a month.

If your revenue goal is $10,000 a month, then you can determine how many sales conversations you need to have every month in order to meet your goal.

How are you going to generate that number of sales conversations? That's where your personal marketing sails in to the rescue. As we mentioned earlier in this book, marketing of any type is the process of generating conversations that might lead to a sale.

So, you would have to do the following every month:

- Book a specific number of face-to-face meetings with members of your network

- Make a certain number of telephone calls

- Spend an hour a day engaging with members of your network on social media (Linked, In, Facebook, Twitter)

- Go to three networking meetings every week and commit to following up with every person of interest through Linked In or a one-to-one meeting

- Post about your networking activity on social media – upload photos of you at the events you attend

- Connect with the people you meet on your social media platforms; Like their Facebook page, if they have one

- Write and post a blog or create an issue of your regular newsletter

- Work on a series of short video posts

- Work on a downloadable white paper that shares valuable information with your ideal clients

- Check in with your website's analytics to see what kind of activity your website is generating and figure out what you need to tweak in order to get people to take the action you would like them to take

- Create a Personal Marketing Plan that identifies the "plays" that you with implement with selected members of your network every month

If that sounds like "overkill," then it might be helpful for you to ask yourself this question: how much of the kind of activity described above are you currently undertaking each week?

How many conversations is your current level of activity generating?

And, the best question of all, how much money are you generating? There is an exponential relationship between the amount of marketing you undertake and the results you get.

More means *MORE*!

And, More almost always means setting goals to help you get there.

There are a lot of theories about how to best set goals but one of the cleanest systems is the "Smart" goal process, where a goal is

S	= Specific
M	= Measurable
A	= Achievable
R	= Realistic
T	= Time-bound

So, in our example above, your goal would be to have a specific number of conversations with prospects every month, let's say five for purposes of illustration.

Let's check in on that.
Is it specific? Yes.

Can you measure that? Yes.

Is it achievable? At a rate of about or two conversations a week, most definitely.

Is it realistic? If you have 40 hours available to you every week with no other impediments, then yes.

And is it time-bound? Yes – those five conversations must be completed within a one-month period.

Here are some other suggestions for maximizing your chances of achieving your goals:

- Make sure you write your goals down

- Visualize what you are going to see, feel, hear and sense when you have achieved your goal

- Share your goals with someone who supports your success

- Carry your written goals around with you

- Take consistent action on your goals

- Reward yourself when you achieve a goal

The more clarity you have around what it is you want to achieve, and the more consistently you take action, the more likely it is that you will create a fulfilling life and successful business. What if you can have almost everything you want...eventually, and as a result of consistent, strategic activity? Start with your goals!

Coaching Note:

Set goals for your business with your coach, making sure you pay specific attention to your revenue goals.

Creating a precise number for your annual revenue every year and tracking those numbers carefully every month with your coach is a very powerful tool for keeping you and your business on track.

The maxim that "you can't manage what you can't measure" is so true.

Some of our best clients embrace their numbers, learn from them all the time, and watch their numbers grow and grow, month to month.

A Referral Marketing Note:

If you choose to integrate referral marketing best practices into your daily habits for creating new business, the above numbers will change.

When you create a high-quality network that is willing to help you by transferring their trust in you, you will find that your referral partners are creating the prospect conversations for you.

Referrals from your trained and committed network will have a much higher closing rate.

Here are some interesting numbers for your consideration:

Average number of referrals needed per month for a strong professional service practice:

2-3 referrals

Where referrals are made by a regular referral partner, they are able to transfer an average amount of trust, and you can expect a 30+% closing rate.

3 referrals = 1 closed deal per month

Where referrals are made by a trained referral marketing partner, they are able to transfer an above-average amount of trust, and you can expect a 60% closing rate.

3 referrals = 2 closed deals per month

Where referrals are made by a trained and committed referral partner, they are able to transfer an exceptional amount of trust, and you can expect closing rates of 80-100%.

3 referrals = 3 closed deals per month

When you receive two-to-three well-qualified referrals per month from your trained network, you can cut your prospecting meetings to a much smaller number.

In order to maintain the flow of referrals that you need to really thrive in your practice or business, you will need to follow all of the goal-setting principles that we've just shared with you.

A suggested method for goal setting for your practice or business employing referral marketing best practices:

Define the number of referrals that you will receive per month from your network

And

Be sure to define the number of referrals that you will be giving per month to your network

For example:

Two referrals monthly given to your network = two referrals that you will receive every month

Yes, it's true! The number of well-placed referrals that you give per month is directly related to the number of referrals that you receive per month.

To quote *The End* by the Beatles:

And in the end

The love you take

Is equal to

The love
You make.

Now that your goals are set, let's go to the fifth rung of the Planning Ladder, which is "Strategies," the epicentre of your Personal Marketing Playbook.

Action You Can Take Today:

Complete the following information:

My annual revenue goal for the year is
_____.

My monthly revenue goal is
_____.

I close one out of every _____ sales calls that I make.

I therefore need to have _____
conversations with prospects every month in order to achieve my monthly goal.

Chapter Eight

Strategies, Actions, Problems, Drama

A PMP Must-Do: Embrace the challenge of creating ongoing social capital, on and off line. Make sure you plan your work week with a minimum of 20 hours per week dedicated to new client development.

Let's circle back to the basic principles of social capital and the opportunity for you to grow your social capital, and your network, every day.

The Simple Truths of Social Capital:

Social capital is the building block of all relationships.

Relationships are the key to all social interactions.

Fundamentally, nothing has really changed since people in caves generated business for one another. It is still all about creating, growing and leveraging social capital for opportunities.

The containers for social capital continue to be the relationships that you develop.

The real story is about the proliferation of tools that now exist for growing social capital–both in the world of referral marketing and content marketing.

In the world of referral marketing, training and coaching is now available on how to create, select and grow the strong relationships from which great referrals can be nurtured.

In fact, there are more than 100 referral marketing strategies and tactics from which to choose!

In the world of content marketing, there are many platforms, tactics and tools that can be used to build further social capital in these relationships. And the list of new tools seems to grow every day.

Back to the Planning Ladder

Let's go back to the Planning Ladder to see where Strategies, Actions, Problems and Drama fit into the picture.

The first Planning Ladder below provides a brief list of Referral Marketing actions or activities you can undertake to further your personal marketing goals.

The second Planning Ladder highlights the corresponding list of Content Marketing activities you can take.

We will bring it all home into one powerful Personal Marketing Playbook Plan template in the last chapter.

The Referral Marketing Planning Ladder

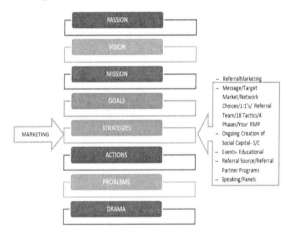

The Planning Ladder

Your new business development success is completely dependent upon your ability to set up the right plan for your activities, based on your own personal style and energy, and to execute on those activities, every...single...day, 20-25 hours every week. Every week of the year.

The beauty of Content Marketing activities is that you can schedule many of your online activities so you can communicate with your network even when you are on vacation.

Content Marketing/On Line Marketing

The Planning Ladder

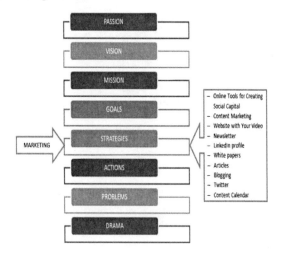

When seasoned sales people talk about the importance of "persistence," it is understood that the ability to maintain your new business development momentum is the key element of revenue success.

Coaching Note:

Establish your Personal Marketing Plan every month and work with your coach to remain accountable.

This ability to continue to execute on vital daily activities ensures you will create clients for the next quarter. Seasoned sales people know that they can never stop their new business activity schedule, as they have experienced the perfect ratio of activity-to-revenue in their business life and they know what it takes to maintain it.

What is the perfect ratio?

New business development energy invested diligently daily = Steady revenue growth

Stick to the plan and you will move mountains!

ACTIONS
A PMP must-do: There are more than 100 referral marketing actions identified in "Chapter 10: Your Playlist of On and Offline Activities." You can take any one of these actions to grow your network and increase the number of powerful referrals you receive.

Spend some time learning about these and select the ones that are most aligned with how you want to do business.

As you know by now, our Personal Marketing Playbook philosophy is based on a combination of Referral marketing and Content Marketing activities.

Many of the Referral Marketing actions you might wish to undertake occur on a face-to-face basis, although catch-up phone calls and follow-up notes with online tools such as LinkedIn are commonly used as well.

The other Personal Marketing Playbook strategy, online Content Marketing, gives you dozens of actions to consider, with more being added to the funnel almost every day.

These actions can be employed to reach out, stimulate and motivate your network on an ongoing basis.

Please see Chapter Ten, Your Playlist, to see the entire collection of on and off line activities that will help you grow your network.

PROBLEMS
A PMPP must do: Prepare for problems. Your coach will help you anticipate them.

You're off to Great Places!
Today is your day!
Your mountain is waiting,
So... get on your way!"
...
So be sure when you step,

Step with care and great tact.
And remember that life's A Great Balancing Act.
And will you succeed?
Yes! You will, indeed!
(98 and ¾ percent guaranteed)
Kid, you'll move mountains!

— **Dr. Seuss, *Oh, The Places You'll Go!***

The "move mountains" imagery from Dr. Seuss's classic children's book, *Oh, The Places You'll Go!* is a good segue into the "Problems" section of the Planning Ladder, as that brilliant author refers to the "prickle-ly places" in which his readers will inevitably find themselves in life.

And to be sure, there will be problems to overcome in maintaining your personal marketing activity schedule. These problems can come in many different, and legitimate, forms. You can be sidetracked by challenges that might include technology, work/life balance, client schedules or the disruptive and welcome demands of onboarding a new client.

131

Throughout your time as a business owner or professional service provider, it is your primary role to "keep your eyes on the prize" and ensure that you do what is **most important** to your business: Do the activities, Do the activities, Do the activities.

And grow, grow, grow your revenue.

Anticipating these inevitable problems or challenges is the best way to address them. The sooner you find solutions to these problems, such as hiring administrative or bookkeeping/accounting resources, the less likely it will be that your energy will be sapped by problems that need not be a part of your daily routine.

Coaching Note:

Be sure that you hold yourself accountable. Your coach will help you reach your goals and ensure that you implement your plans.

DRAMA

A PMPP must do: Identify the areas of drama in your life that are preventing you from focusing profoundly on your personal marketing activities. And then do whatever you can to minimize or eliminate them.

There is one more rung on the ladder to be considered and that is the "Drama" rung. Drama refers to people, behaviours (yours or theirs) or activities that do not serve you and, therefore, nor your business.

Your collection of "drama" items needs to be appropriately and peacefully settled in order for you to move forward smoothly and comfortably with your new business development routine.

Examples of "Drama" may be found in a long list of miseries including difficult relationships at the office or at home, unprocessed negative experiences and, of course, there are the Saboteurs.

What are the Saboteurs?

The Saboteurs are negative thoughts or fears that plague professional service providers or business owners when they don't generate the revenue that they deserve, or don't know how to create the revenue that they dearly would like to have.

Paula has written a book, edited by Susan, on this topic, called, *Stop the Saboteurs: Conquer Negative Thoughts that Hurt your Revenue and Your Brand.*[9]

---

[9] https://amzn.to/2YHuauN

Whatever the source of the "Drama," every business owner or professional service provider must manage these devils in order that they may execute on what is most important to the lifeblood of their business.

Find out how well you are managing your own saboteurs through the Saboteur Self-Assessment Quiz on Paula's website at: YourPmp-Hope.com

Do the activities that feed the revenue of the business. Nothing can be more important to your business than personal marketing activities.

Coaching Note:

Your coach can help you manage the drama in your life. His/her role is to make sure that drama does not prevent you from reaching your full potential.

And herein lies the key reason why every business owner or professional service provider hires a coach.

With all of the competing priorities in a business leader's life, they must be able to choose wisely, every day, about how to best invest their time.

It is so easy to choose an important family event over a key networking event, rather than make a plan that ensures you are able to manage both.

Coaches are available to support you with your referral marketing and your online content marketing activities.

Although you can hire people to help you create some of your content, supporting your referral network partners online is something that is best done by you, personally.

And it pretty much goes without saying that your referral marketing activities are based solely on the personal exposure and support to your network that only you can provide.

The Planning Ladder has formed the backbone of your business or practice.

Now it's time to take the steps that will lead to creating the daily activity plan that will truly grow your business. And ensure that you are enjoying your new business development activities!

Ready? *Onward!*

PART THREE: THE EXPEDITION BEGINS

Chapter Nine:
Taking Your First Personal Marketing Steps and Continuing to Climb

Chapter Nine
To Base Camp and Beyond!

A PMP Must-Do: Don't Look Down. Or Back.

Getting started with any project (and maintaining momentum) can be challenging and that's part of the magic and the misery of creation: it's all up to you.

Somehow, you have to pull information out of the void and organize it into a package of productive actions that are going to make you money.

Just as Mount Everest can't be climbed in an hour, Personal Marketing success doesn't happen overnight. It takes plenty of consistent effort rolled out over a long period of time to reach the summit.

During that time, it's important that you don't look down and don't look back. Stay focused on getting to the top—where some amazing results await you—and you will get there!

The previous sections of this book have been focused on filling your rucksack with the tools you'll need to summit.

139

Now let's check to make sure you've got those tools handy, and start gathering steam as you work towards your goal!

Some of the steps we've outlined in the following pages might seem to repeat some of the information we've laid out earlier and that's OK: we wanted to collect the most important information all in one section so that you can move forward powerfully on the magnificent project of succeeding with your personal marketing.

Now, without further ado, *let's go*!

Pinnacle Point #1:

Stratify Your Relationships

This is where the rubber *really* starts hitting the road. Your Personal Marketing Playbook Plan is a vehicle by which you can organize your relationships into one of the three phases of a budding referral relationship.

Once you know which members of your network fit into which phase, you can then identify which of the personal marketing playbook plays, or tactics, you would like to use to advance your relationships.

You will be amazed at all of the plays that are available to you—there are more than 100 altogether! You will find the full playlist later in Chapter Ten in this book in the section called "Your Playlist of Powerful Personal Marketing Activities."

Dr. Ivan Misner, founder of the well-known Business Network International (BNI) networking groups, and bestselling business author, Daniel Pink, use similar rubrics to assess referral relationships:

Phase 1 Relationships

Phase 1 relationships involve those members of your network who "like and trust" you but know nothing about your business.

141

They represent approximately 88% of your network. You are visible to them, but no more than that. Can you see why most members of your network are not giving you referrals? They don't know enough about you.

Phase 2 Relationships

Phase 2 relationships imply a deeper stage of connection than Phase 1 relationships, in that you have credibility with the people in this category.

Roughly 10% of a typical business professional's network fall into this category and they fulfill the following criteria,

- They know, like and trust you

- They have knowledge of your business. Ideally, they can answer five basic questions about you: What do you do? What are your products and services? Who do you serve? What's unique about you? And why do you love what you do?

- They have generated **leads** for you (opportunities without any transfer of trust) *e.g. "I know that my friend/ family member is struggling financially with their business... please call them about your factoring services but don't use my name."*

- They may even have generated referrals that are generated when a need is presented by a network member

  e.g. "I would like to tell you about my colleague in the factoring profession. I believe that s/he can help you pay for the material for that new piece of business that you are worried about.

  Let me introduce you to her or him some time."

Phase 3 Relationships
The ultimate relationships from a personal marketing standpoint represent only 2% of a typical business professional's network.

These are the relationships that are actually *profitable* for you, and they fulfill the following criteria:

- They exhibit all of the traits of a Phase 2 relationship: high trust levels, knowledge of one another's business, they can answer all of the five key questions about your business, and they have generated leads and referrals for you

- **Plus...They are raving fans.** They believe that you have a very special service or product and they do not hesitate to initiate conversations on your behalf...

143

- **_And_ they create proactive referrals.**
  e.g. _"In case you do get that big order that you were telling me about, I want to introduce you to my colleague in the factoring profession, who can make sure that you are ready for the business before your customer makes the decision. Let's all three of us have a coffee together next week."_

Here's what the Three Stages of a Referral Relationship look like if we imagine them as part of your business development funnel:

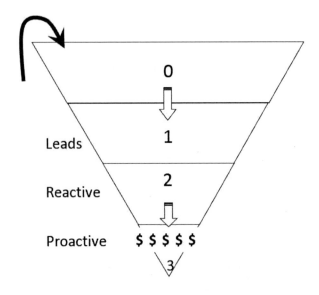

Take a few minutes right now to stratify your relationships.

In the next few pages, we're giving you the space to write down the names of the people with whom you have Phase 1, Phase 2 and Phase 3 relationships.

We'll tell you more about how to use that information next.

If you would prefer, please go to either:

YourPmp-Crossman.com or YourPmp-Hope.com   and access your Personal Marketing Playbook Plan online. It will help you to place all of your referral relationships into four different categories.

Why four categories when there are only three stages of a referral relationship?

Because every business professional needs to capture the relationships that are in the stage before trust is created.

We call this primary stage "Phase 0."

Phase 0 Relationships: Refer to a *New Relationship – No Trust has Been Established Yet – They Know Nothing about your Business!*

The people I know who are in this phase of relationship with me are:

_____

_____

_____

_____

_____

_____

_____

_____

_____

_____

_____

_____

Phase 1 Relationships: Refer to *Established*

Relationships – They Know, Like and Trust You – And Know Nothing about your Business – yet!

The people I know who are in this phase of relationship with me are:

_____

_____

_____

_____

_____

_____

_____

_____

_____

_____

_____

Phase 2 Relationships: Refer to *Well-Established Relationships – people Know, Like and Trust You – they Know Your Business and Have Confidence in You and Your Business*

The people I know who are in this phase of relationship with me are:

_____

_____

_____

_____

_____

_____

_____

_____

_____

_____

_____

_____

_____

Phase 3 Relationships: *Your Raving Fans – they Know, Like and Trust You, Know your Business, Have a Strong Belief in You and Your Business and Are Proactive about Promoting You*

The people I know who are in this phase of relationship with me are:

_____

_____

_____

_____

_____

_____

_____

_____

_____

_____

_____

_____

_____

That's an interesting process, isn't it?

Do you see some patterns?

Do you find that you have a lot of relationships in the Phase 0 and Phase 1 category?

Did you also find that you have fewer than 10 relationships in Phase 2?

And that you have 0-5 relationships in Phase 3?

The Biggest Secret in Personal Marketing

Now that you've stratified your relationships, we're going to share with you the biggest secret in personal marketing: to get the most bang for your social capital buck, we strongly recommend that you focus your energy both on and offline on selected relationships.

We call them your golden relationships and they lie in the Phase 2 and Phase 3 layers of your network. The people in these categories are going to become your referral partners— perhaps some of them already are!

Thinking about the power of Phase 3 relationships always puts me in mind of the movie, **Julia**, starring Jane Fonda and Vanessa Redgrave. In the movie, Julia and Lillian enjoy a close relationship in childhood and beyond, and eventually Julia goes on to an illustrious life as a physician with anti-Nazi sympathies. Lillian strikes it big as a celebrated playwright.

When Lillian is invited to a writer's conference in Russia in pre-World War 11 Europe, Julia enlists her assistance to smuggle money through Nazi Germany to support the effort to fight the Nazis. It is a dangerous mission, especially for a Jewish intellectual on her way to Russia...

Calls to action don't get much more demanding. Asking a Jewish playwright to bring money into Nazi Germany to help with the anti-Nazi cause? It is a "dangerous" mission, indeed!

Foolhardy, some would say.

And Lillian does it.

Because her friend asked her.

And so it goes with those who are in deep referral relationships, in Phase 3 relationships, where both members of the relationship are committed to one another's mutual prosperity and gain.

Here are but a few examples of Phase 3 relationships that Paula has seen reap amazing results. Partners who:

- Brainstorm, support and execute monthly, for a period of years, to ensure that a dream is fulfilled

- Set one another up for the deal of their lives with the right connections and encouragement

- Are the only financial resources to step up when all others say, "no"

- Who dig deep to find a resource to help their partner, even when they cannot afford it

- They can be called up to "fill in" for their referral partner, at the last minute, when they are not able to deliver services due to an emergency or health issues

The only real limitation to a Phase 3 Relationship? *Isolating and making the request that will really help the Phase 3 Partner's world*

...Ask one another, what is the number one action that the Phase 3 partner can perform to advance their referral partner's business? Line up a speaking engagement with their target market? Host a seminar on their behalf? Hold a joint event? Promote their services in a newsletter?

Because anything is possible in a Phase 3 relationship. Put differently, you can ask your Phase 3 referral partner to do anything for you.

They represent the most powerful opportunities that you have available. It is up to you to make the right request!

And where do many business professionals invest their valuable personal marketing time? In Phase 0 relationships, where there is no trust established and no trust that can be transferred. And, yet, referrals, where trust is transferred, is the life blood of their business.

Is there an opportunity for you to focus on your key relationships, your Phase 2 and Phase 3 relationships, to grow your business, on and off line? We think so.

Pinnacle Point # 2:

How You Are Going to Invite People to Work with You?

Once you know who fits where in your network, who your ideal client is, and what you do for them, it's vital that you become very clear on how you will invite them to work with you.

You need to educate your referral partners about how you do this, as well.

Do you offer service packages for which people can register?

Or online training programs?

Do people work with you one-on-one or in groups?

Do you have products they can buy, or a book that will show highlights of your knowledge, philosophy or personality?

The more clarity you can offer around how people can access your business offering, the more likely they are to buy from you. Your referral sources/partners and prospects are going to be reading or viewing your content online and you want to provide them with a clear process for working with you:

- Do you offer them a free consultation, so you can determine how (or if) you can help them?

- Do you want them to fill out a short survey to clarify how (or if) you can serve them?

- Should they email or call you or your assistant directly to book their first call?

Your content should always contain a clear Call to Action (CTA) that invites people to take a specific step that will result in a closer relationship with you.

Sometimes your CTA will simply be to sign up for your free newsletter. Sometimes it will be to book a free consultation. Or download your free whitepaper on a topic of relevance to your ideal client (which itself should include another Call to Action) Usually people have to land on a page on your website in order to answer your call to action.

Know what action you want people to take and embed a clear CTA in each piece of content, and in your spoken message. Success begins with directing traffic to where you want your network and prospects to go when they want help from you. Make this part very easy for your ideal client!!!

Remember: marketing is all about starting conversation with the people with whom you want to do business. How, specifically, can they get into conversation with you?

My Calls to Action Are:

1. _____

2. _____

3. _____

Pinnacle Point #3:

Develop a Personal Marketing Plan

Ideally you want to wrap all of your personal marketing initiatives into a logical strategy that summarizes and guides your personal marketing programs, pinpointing the tools that are most likely to resonate with your target audience. This is a big piece.

And it's going to change over time. The goals of a personal marketing plan are to:

1. Increase your business visibility –both on and offline

2. Communicate your—and your business's —unique strengths and attributes, as perceived by your ideal customer

3. Tell the stories that demonstrate your— and your business's—values and culture

4. Differentiate your business from others in its niche

5. Increase lead generation and, most important of all,

6. Support the members of your referral network

The tools you might use to do this include:

- Your business card, developed to resonate with you and your target market

- All of the 40 + actions on the Booked Solid by Referral Scorecard (these actions are found at: YourPmp-Hope.com

- A regular blog

- A newsletter

- A downloadable white paper

- An email program

- Social media

- Informational videos

- Case studies about the problems you solve

- Your fully optimized LinkedIn profile

- Your website, which, ultimately, should be designed to support all of your personal marketing endeavours

Write it all down! You want to itemize all of the ways you are going to lead people to the business portal that will start up a conversation so you don't forget a single thing! The results available through your personal marketing efforts tend to develop over time as news about you percolates through your network.

The point of creating a personal marketing program is to generate more business, and this takes time. This is no "quick fix" initiative.

The Level of Trust

Whether you are focusing on your online or offline efforts, results from reaching out to your network are tied to the level of trust that you enjoy with the people in it, the quality of your message about your target market and, finally, your ability to relate effectively with referral sources who will connect you with your ideal client.

Since these elements can be difficult to define for most business professionals or owners, you may not be able to predict the arrival time of their referrals – at first.

As you become better trained in referral marketing techniques, predictability becomes more readily available.

Blocking Your Time

Your monthly Personal Marketing Playbook Plan helps you block all of your online, networking and referral-building activities all in one place. Try to develop your plan a few weeks before the new month arrives.

A general rule of thumb is to balance your week with:

1. One-two hours every day of daily social media activities to stimulate growth in your social capital with selected members of your network members (use your "Personal Marketing Playlist" in Chapter Ten) as your key resource for next steps.

2. Two-to-three formal networking events weekly, strategically selected according to the clear definition of your target market, where either prospective referral sources or actual prospects for your business will be present for connecting opportunities. Plus, two-to three 1:1 "coffee" meetings, every week, with selected or new members of your network.

3. You can use your electronic or paper calendars, or a CRM system to organize your time commitments. Use the method that works best for you.

But the key point is to write it all down and formalize the commitments you make to your personal marketing.

From a content marketing perspective, you'll want to develop an editorial calendar in tandem with your networking and personal meeting calendar. And what is an editorial calendar?

It's a schedule that sets out what content you are going to post to your online properties, and when, so you can be methodical and consistent in your content-related behavior.

For example, what blog posts are you going to create this month, and when will they be posted?

How are you going to be supporting them on social media, and when?

Will you be deploying a monthly email to alert your network of a new post?

How are you going to be supporting members of your network online?

Does a referral partner have an important event coming up this month that you would like to promote on their behalf?

An ad hoc approach to content creation and curation is not going to cut it. It's too easy to get busy doing other things. You are building relationships and relationships require consistent attention. And consistent attention generally means a schedule has to be in play.

Sample Calendar of Content Marketing Activities:

Sunday	Monday	Tuesday	Wednesday	Thursday	Friday	Saturday
1/ 30 minutes Social Media Support of Referral Network; 30 minutes Commenting on Linked In Groups	2/ Work on drafting downloadable White Paper for Website (1 hr.) 30 minutes on social media	3/ Post Blog Support blog on Social Media Email blast to network re: blog 30 minutes on social media	4/ Work on drafting downloadable White Paper for Website (1 hr.) 30 minutes on social media	5/ Work on drafting downloadable White Paper for Website (1 hr.) 30 minutes on social media	6/ Work on drafting downloadable White Paper for Website (1 hr.) 30 minutes on social media	7/ Draft next week's blog Work on drafting downloadable White Paper for Website (1 hr.)
8/ 30 minutes Social Media Support of Referral Network; 30 minutes Commenting on Linked In Groups	9/ Work on drafting downloadable White Paper for Website (1 hr.) 30 minutes on social media	10/ Post Blog Support blog on Social Media Email blast to network re: blog 30 minutes on social media	11/ Work on drafting downloadable White Paper for Website (1 hr.) 30 minutes on social media	12/ Work on drafting downloadable White Paper for Website (1 hr.) 30 minutes on social media	13/ Work on drafting downloadable White Paper for Website (1 hr.) 30 minutes on social media	14/ Work on drafting downloadable White Paper for Website (1 hr.) Draft next week's blog
15/ 30 minutes Social Media Support of Referral Network; 30 minutes Commenting on Linked In Groups	16/ Proof graphic design for White Paper 30 minutes on social media	17/ Post Blog Support blog on Social Media Email blast to network re: blog 30 minutes on social media	18/ Send White Paper to web developer to upload to website 30 minutes on social media	19/ Plan online promotional campaign for white paper 30 minutes on social media	20/ Plan online promotional campaign for white paper 30 minutes on social media	21/ Draft next week's blog
22/ 30 minutes Social Media Support of Referral Network; 30 minutes Commenting on Linked In Groups	23/ Execute on promotional plan for white paper 30 minutes on social media	24/ Post Blog Support blog on Social Media Email blast to network re: blog 30 minutes on social media	25/ Execute on promotional plan for white paper 30 minutes on social media	26/ Execute on promotional plan for white paper 30 minutes on social media	27/ Fine tune social media profiles so they are more accurate and more effectively represent your brand 30 minutes on social media	28/ Draft next week's blog

Need Resources to Find Out More?

Search the internet and you will find an enormous number of resources aimed at helping you with your content marketing initiatives.

There truly are a lot of fabulous sites run by some very knowledgeable people who can provide you with more free information that will help you learn more about how to do all this yourself. Susan's own personal favourites include:

- **Hubspot**
  hubspot.com
- **The Content Marketing Institute**
  contentmarketinginstitute.com
- **Copyblogger**
  copyblogger.com
- **Quick Sprout**
  quicksprout.com

Note from Paula: Or consider hiring Susan! She and her team can ensure that you have maximized your online presence and all the marketing opportunities that await you online!

Pinnacle Point #4:

Get Out of Your Office and Network/Connect Consistently with Your Referral Sources

Even though it's vital to stratify your relationships and know who is meeting you at which phase of relationship development, you still need to be networking.

As we mentioned previously, you need to attend two-to-three networking events and have two-to-three face-to-face meetings with members of your network every week.

You can supplement (but not replace!) this activity by connecting with all of the key people in your network online so that you can support them on social media as appropriate.

The most important platform for most business professionals currently is Linked In. Once you're connected to people on this platform, make sure you "follow" them, and their company page, if they have one, as well.

This advice holds true for referral partners, as well as for people whose business you would like to earn, by the way.

Make it a habit to:

- Endorse your referral sources for the skills you feel they possess
- Give them a recommendation
- "Like" and "Share" the content they are posting to their news feed
- Comment on their status updates and any articles they share in their news feed that resonate with you
- Ask to join any groups they are hosting, if it is appropriate
- Post to your own news stream as well, and ask your referral source to support your content by liking, commenting and sharing any posts that resonate with them as well
- Post any articles you've written to Linked In Pulse by hitting the "Share an Article" button in your status update box. This raises your visibility on Linked In
- Suggest to your referral partners that they message you if they want you to support one of their posts – for example, they might like you to share registration information for an upcoming event on your social media platforms. You can make similar requests of them.

- Get in the habit of connecting with any great contacts you meet at networking events. Use autoresponder technology to help with sign-ups to your "next step" vehicles such as your newsletter or blogs.

And, of course, the LinkedIn invitation tool is very helpful with creating next steps with network members.

Remember we suggested the idea of an editorial calendar? Here's where scheduling your time online pays off. It's consistent, orderly effort that is going to take you across the finish line. Get cracking!

Pinnacle Point #5:

Dive into the Joys of Thought Leadership

Focusing on your own thought leadership activities and that of the members of your referral network represents a key opportunity for succeeding in your personal marketing.

Keep your ear to the ground so you don't miss hearing about the successes of the members of your network. Have they written a book? Promote it on and offline! Have they been hired for a key project? Tell other people how amazing they are. Do they have a blog? Share it online through your business's own social media networks.

In fact, blogging is an important activity for enhancing your own thought leadership, as well. Get into the habit of blogging – even if you can only manage it once a month – and "Like" and "Share" your referral partners' blog posts, if they are writing them.

Some people will post a link to their blog posts on their social media feeds, and/or post them to LinkedIn Pulse.

You can search through your referral partners' Linked In, Twitter, Facebook or other news feeds to find a link back to the website where they are hosting the post, or you can navigate directly to their website, and search for their latest blog (usually there is a "Blog" tab on their website). Most blogs have administrators who filter any comments received, so if you do comment, be prepared to wait for it to show up online. Some platforms also require you to create an account and sign in before you can post a comment. You might also:

- Ask your referral partners to read your blog posts and like, share and comment on any that inspire them so to do.
- Offer to write a guest blog for any referral partners where this might be a good fit (and make sure you provide links to your guest blog through social media)

- If you have a blog, invite your referral partners to write a guest blog post for your own audience

By the Way...Make Sure You Post Content with Strong Visuals

Including images and videos in your content adds excitement and increases visitor engagement. Text is a great way to tell your story, but remember that a picture tells a thousand words and video brings emotion into the mix as well.

They both help you tell a more powerful story. There are a number of stock image sites, like Dreamstime, Bigstock and iStock that enable you to purchase the right to use an image for commercial purchases. It can take some time to find just the "right" image to use, but it's well worth the search.

A Word About Stories....

People love stories, so get into the habit of telling your business story in engaging ways, both in your face-to-face networking and online. You might share the story of why you started your business, or the story of how you developed a new product or service.

You might tell the story of how you solved a tricky problem for a client or customer, or the story of how your industry has changed over the past five or 10 years. The sky's the limit!

Here's a rubric that will help you quickly come up with nine blog topics:

My Clients' 3 Biggest Problems:	One Solution I Offer:	Another Solution I Offer:	A Third Solution I Offer:
1.			
2.			
3.			

Pinnacle Point #6:
Be Strategic: Execute on Referral-Building Tactics to Advance Your Personal Marketing Activities

There are almost 20 tactics that business professionals can use to consciously advance their relationships to the next level.

Most of these tactics can be extended successfully to online methods which also advance relationships when these tactics, or plays, are deliberately employed with selected high value relationships.[10]

Different tactics, or plays, will resonate with different individual business professionals. Here are four examples of classic tactics, or "plays," that might work for you, on and offline, to advance your key relationships:

1. **Connecting** – Make a habit of connecting as many members of your network with one another as possible.

---

[10] See the book, *Business by Referral A Sure Fire Way to Generate New Business,* for more on referral marketing tactics -- Misner, Ivan R. (Ph.D.) and Davis, Robert, Business by Referral, Bard Press, Austin, Texas, 1998

They will appreciate your efforts and will reciprocate with creating connections for you.

What goes around truly comes around. You can connect members of your network through email, LinkedIn, and many other platforms.

And, of course, connecting can be done over a coffee or a beer!

2. **Advising** - When you are a professional service provider, sharing your advice can become a valuable gift that you can share freely with selected members of your network. Advising is a way by which your network can "experience" the method and delivery of your advice.

Advising can be done electronically through a newsletter or email format or, of course, during a casual dinner. One caveat: Be sure to turn off the advice tap when you are in front of a prospect who is ready to *pay* for your advice.

3. **Inviting** - Inviting members of your network to events is a very good habit to develop. When you see there's an exciting speaker at your local chamber

or networking group, be sure to invite valued members of your network to join you at the event.

Your generosity will not be forgotten, and you will start the reciprocal process of being invited to various events where you can expand your network. Inviting can be done on or off line as well.

4. **Collaborating** - Collaborating with members of your network to develop business opportunities for one another is one of the most effective plays for growing your business.

   When you are in a Phase 3 relationship where the two of you are committed to growing one another's business, there is no better way to invest your time than collaborating with your referral partner to plan an event, find speaking opportunities for each other or creating a plan for approaching a key prospect.

   With all of the trust, goodwill and belief in one another's businesses present in a solid referral partnership, collaborating will bear the most fruit for all parties.

Other tactics or plays that you may consider for on or off line applications might include:

5. **Advice Seeking** – Most business professionals will appreciate your wanting to know more about their practice by seeking their advice.

6. **Volunteering** – When you are looking to grow a relationship, volunteer to help your contact develop an important project.

7. **Recruiting** – Bring a valued member of your network onto a board or committee that would resonate with them.

8. **Reporting** – Interview a member of your network for an article, blog or white paper.

9. **Announcing** – You can help members of your network move their business forward by announcing events personally or online.

10. **Recognizing** – Be sure to use every opportunity to recognize members of your network when they have received an award or any other form of recognition

11. **Horn Tooting** – Yes, please do toot your own horn so members of your network will promote you with pride

12. **Promoting** – You can actively promote members of your network during a networking event or any online vehicle

13. **Purchasing** – Your network member will never forget if you purchase his/her book. All the better for you and your relationship if you reach out and purchase even larger services from them.

14. **Shopping Around** – You might want to seek the advice of members of your network in the spirit of "shopping around." You will need to make it clear that you are in a process of finding out if you require the service.

15. **Source Seeking** – You can turn to members of your network in your search for finding a particular source for valuable information.

16. **Sponsoring** – There are always opportunities to sponsor members of your network when they are supporting good causes. Or when members of your network are

launching a book or creating their own event.

17. **Researching** – You can ask members of your network to help you with a research project. They will become aware of the benefits of working with you during the course of the research.

18. **Auditing** – Asking a member of your network to try out a product, review a case study or comment on a new service is an excellent method to deepen your relationship with them.

Please see the playlist in Chapter 10 to help you implement any one of these referral-building tactics available to you.

Note from Susan: If you want to know more about how to put these tactics to work for you, ask Paula to show you the way!"

A Special Reminder about Online Plays

You can weave both online and offline actions around every one of these tactics – for example, you can like and share content created by the members of your referral network on any of the social media platforms on which you are connected with them (and you should be connected with them on all of them!).

You can even suggest to members of your network that they message you if they want you to support one of their posts—for an upcoming event for which they would like registrations for example, or an announcement.

You can make similar requests of them.

Generally speaking, the principles of doing this are going to be pretty much the same for Linked In, Facebook, Twitter, Instagram, Pinterest (or likely any other social media platform that becomes popular after this book is published!):

- Like your referral partner's company page wherever they have one
- Follow or connect with them on each platform
- Like and share their posts and
- Give impromptu shout-outs to them on a regular basis

Pinnacle Point #7:

Step Into the Spotlight with Events, Speaking Engagements and Panel Participation

While our focus in this book is to emphasize how to connect powerfully with the members of your referral network, you want to make sure that your community presence, online and offline, indicates that you are "Open for Business."

This may be harder for people who are more introverted than others but, trust us, there are ways to do this in a way that respects your comfort level either way. Hosting events, speaking to audiences that are made up of your potential clients or customers, and participating in panels of experts in your field are all great habits to cultivate that will get you known in your field.

Telling people that you are doing these things through the online platforms you control will let even more people know that you are an expert at what you do.

Tell your potential customers how to get their questions answered, show them how to obtain more information about your product or service, provide your contact information and, more than anything, give them the next step in the process of getting to know whether you are a good fit for what they are looking for.

You don't need to knock people over with opportunities – but you do need to make it obvious how they can deepen the conversation if that is what they would like to do. Here are some suggestions for doing that:

- Hold an annual event and invite members of your network, and your clients, to attend
- Support your event through online activities
- Connect selected members of your network with speaking engagement opportunities
- Recommend selected members of your network as panelists in relevant learning forums
- Invite people to comment on your blog
- Invite people to comment on an issue you have raised in one of your status updates or in a group on Linked In
- Encourage people to contact you with questions

PART FOUR: SUMMITING

Chapter Ten:
Your Personal Marketing Playbook Playlist and Plan

Chapter Ten:
Your Personal Marketing Playbook Playlist of Marketing Activities

A PMP Must-Do: Choose the Plays that resonate with you.

Are you ready to put your favourite plays into your Personal Marketing Playbook Plan? You will find a useful template for your Personal Marketing Plan on both Susan's and Paula's websites. It will help you organize your Phase 0, 1, 2, 3 relationships and the plays that you want to plan with each one:

YourPmp-Crossman.com

YourPmp-Hope.com

Here's how to use the PMP template:

1. Access the Personal Marketing Play-book Plan from our websites
2. Complete the "Relationships" section by placing the names of members of your network into the relevant category. Are they in the 0, 1, 2 or 3 categories?

3. Review the playlist activities in this chapter and choose an activity that will advance every relationship that you have identified.
4. Give yourself a deadline by which each activity needs to be completed.

There are a lot of choices available to you in developing your Personal Marketing Playbook Plan, and you want to be sure that you choose the plays that resonate with you and with the network member that you have selected.

Think of it this way: if you are having fun with your plays, you will continue to choose and execute on them – every day. Daily personal marketing plays will create the revenue you deserve!

Remember, it takes consistent action over time to succeed. Success typically doesn't happen overnight. Or likely in the first month.

You need to turn personal marketing into a way of life and stay in action continuously, day after day, month after month, year after year. This might all seem quite unfamiliar in the beginning.

However, as you stick to your plan, you'll start to see results and you'll become ever more motivated to keep up the great work on the personal marketing front.

This section of the book summarizes all of the PM plays that you can make with your network members. It is a handy list of plays to which you can refer any time you need a refresher.

And look how many plays there are on this list! 103 plays from which to choose! And you can add plays of your own, too, once you get going.

Your Personal Marketing Plays:

1. Give a referral to a member of your network

5. Give someone a recommendation for online and printed material usage

6. Create a 1:1 in-depth meeting with Phase 1 network member

7. Create a 1:1 in-depth meeting with Phase 2 network member

8. Create a 1:1 in-depth meeting with Phase 3 network member

9. Face-to-Face Tactics: Volunteering, Recruiting, Researching

10. Face-to-Face Tactics: Reporting, Source Seeking, Advice Seeking

11. Face-to-Face Tactics: Advising, Announcing, Shopping Around

12. Face-to-Face Tactics: Purchasing, Connecting, Inviting

13. Face-to-Face Tactics: Recognizing, Horn Tooting, Sponsoring

14. Face-to-Face Tactics: Promoting, Auditing

15. Face-to-Face Tactic: Collaborating with a network member

16. Online Tactics: Researching, Source Seeking, Announcing

17. Online Tactics: Shopping Around, Purchasing, Connecting

18. Online Tactics: Inviting, Recognizing, Horn Tooting, Sponsoring

19. Online Tactics: Promoting, Auditing

20. Attend a strategically chosen Networking event

21. Create an Activity with max. four people, 1 hr/person (golf, tennis, cards)

22. Arrange a speaking engagement for a network member

23. Arrange an online podcast interview for a network member

24. Set up an advisory board

25. Prepare a written testimonial/for a network member - on/off line

26. Include a network member in your newsletter or your website

27. Make a phone call to a network member simply to connect with them

28. Direct message a network member simply to say "hello!"

29. Send an article of interest to a network member

30. Nominate a network member for a new role

31. Create a written and signed agreement for a valued network member

32. Develop and execute on an Education Seminar Event with members of your network

33. Invite a network member to join you on an online webinar to showcase their expertise

34. Promote one of your events through online activities

35. Design a group activity for your own and a network member's clients

36. Connect with all Referral Sources on Linked In

37. Execute on blogging-related activities (yours and others)

38. Like and share a referral source's content

39. Connect selected members of your network with speaking engagement opportunities

40. Recommend selected members of your network as panelists in relevant learning forums

41. Invite people to comment on your blog

42. Invite people to comment on an issue you have raised in one of your status updates or in a group on Linked In

43. Invite members of your network to download any free content you have available on your website

44. Invite members of your network, to download any free content a referral partner has on their website

45. Share a recommendation or endorse your referral sources for the skills you feel they possess

46. "Like" and "share" content that members of your network are posting to their news feed

47. Comment on status updates and any articles shared in the news feed of selected members of your network

48. Ask to join any groups your network members are hosting

49. Post to your own news stream and ask your referral source to support your content by liking, commenting and sharing any posts that resonate with them

50. Post any articles you've written to Linked In Pulse by hitting the "Share an Article" button in your status update box. This action gives you a thought leadership profile, raising your visibility in the Linked In database.

51. Suggest to your referral partners that they message you if they want you to support one of their posts – for example, for an upcoming event for which they would like registrations. You can make similar requests of them. They are your referral partner!

52. Get in the habit of connecting with any great contacts you meet at networking events.

53. Use autoresponder technology to help with sign-ups to your "next step" vehicles such as your newsletter or blogs.

54. The LinkedIn invitation tool is very helpful in creating next steps with network members.

55. Like your referral partner's company page wherever they have one

56. Follow or connect with your referral sources and partners on each platform

57. Give impromptu shout-outs to network members on a regular basis

58. Introduce members of your network that you want to help with other members of your network who you also like and trust

59. Bring valued members of your network together as much as you possibly can

60. Praise your colleagues at networking events as you make connections together

61. Amplify a speaker in your network, by tweeting to their network as you watch them in action

62. Ask a member of your network who shares your target market about their business. Listen carefully to their answer.

You might want to have a coffee together to discuss how you can help one another

63. Connect valued members of your network with other valued members of your network.

64. Help valued members of your network with an introduction to a highly important Prospect

65. Provide feedback on their corporate direction or materials

66. Share a highly confidential problem and request their assistance with it

67. Ask them to join a strategic committee for their business

68. Create a new network group which is comprised of service providers with a common target market

69. Invite referral sources/partners to announce new programs to trusted members on their LinkedIn network.

70. Cross-promote your referral source's program or offer between platforms e.g. from LinkedIn to Twitter

71. Upload images you took of you and your referral partner at an event you or they had held – tag them in the photos

72. Share the specific target market details that direct your referral sources to an opportunity for you

73. Share time with a prospect and your referal partner by attending a meeting with the prospect to ensure a solid outcome for both of you

74. Share feedback of the needs of a prospect in order that your referral partner is well-prepared to move forward during their upcoming meeting with them

75. Share an experience with a prospect about your referral partner's programs that serves as a strong testimonial during any meetings you have with them

76. With Phase 3 relationships, you can ask for any help that you require

77. Ask your referral partners to read your blog posts and like, share and comment on any that inspire them so to do

78. Offer to write a guest blog for any referral partners where this might be a good fit (and make sure you provide links to your guest blog through social media)

79. Ask your referral partners who they know who could be good candidates for writing a guest blog for you

80. Ask your referral partners who they know who shares good online content relevant to your target audience that you could make available to your own online community

81. Support your referral partners by linking to any online news that might benefit their business

82. Support your referral partners by looking for online opportunities that might benefit their business or their target audience

83. Collaborate with your referral partners to any goal or end

84. Share a referral partner's blog with your network, giving an introduction identifying their ideal client and desired call to action

85. Think Quality over Quantity when evaluating network members and networking events

86. Ask about the needs of your referral partners' prospects and the special solutions they provide to their prospect's problems. Listen carefully for

their answers and think about a "reactive referral" you can provide.

87. Develop a great recommendation that they can add to their LinkedIn profile

88. Ask your referral partner to help you with a strategic request

89. Provide your referral partner with a heartfelt testimonial

90. Ask them to announce your new programs to trusted members of their LinkedIn network

91. Ask them to forward an email to their network members, with a specific call to action about your offer

92. Communicate your Ask with a Story to help your network explain your services to their network

93. Express gratitude in any way that works for you. A thank you card, a small personal gift, wine always works!

94. Reward selected members of your network when they have been helpful to you

95. Honour your referral partners in your online newsletter

96. Promote your referral partner's business offer or upcoming event in a special emailing to your Database

97. Encourage members of your online community to sign up for your referral partners' Database

98. Ask your referral partners to promote any livestreaming projects you undertake

99. If your business has its own mobile app, ask your referral partners to promote it to their network; do the same for them

100. Ask your referral partners to subscribe to your YouTube video channel

101. Subscribe to your referral partners' YouTube video channels

102. Offer to provide a video testimonial for your referral partner's company video project

103. Be on constant alert for ways to support your referral partners online or offline!

We invite you to add your own special plays to the list as you develop your unique approach to growing your referral sources/partners – and your network!

Are you ready to launch or re-launch yourself into the networking world?

Part Five of Your PMP is designed to help you with that lofty task of hosting a launch event for your business.

This is an important way to tell your world that you are "open for business" and ready to celebrate and extend the relationships you have with the people in your network.

Have a look at the day-by-day list in the next chapter that we developed for your vital on and offline plays for your business.

PART FIVE: ONBOARDING YOUR BUSINESS WITH PERSONAL MARKETING

A Sample of Twelve Weeks of Activity

Onboarding Your Business with Personal Marketing:

A Sample of Twelve Weeks of Activity

Now that you have the basics under your belt, let's see what this would look like in real life. We know that luck plays a part in every business endeavour, but if you want to really hit a home run you need to make a plan and work your plan.

To help you out, we've put together a checklist of recommended activities, with timelines, for generating online and offline success with your personal marketing during your first 90 days of opening a business.

Don't worry if your reality doesn't match these suggestions. It isn't always easy to become a personal marketing virtuoso. But it is always rewarding.

We know it takes a lot of work to profit from your personal marketing efforts. Building a business can be lonely work, and friends and family members don't always understand your mission or your drive to complete it.

The best advice we can offer is to hold fast to your dream, build the best strategy you can create, and seek advice when necessary. If you would like more advice on your personal marketing endeavours, please feel free to connect with us. Our contact details are at the end of the book. Note that the full playbook plan template is available at either of our two website at: YourPmp-Crossman.com or YourPmp-Hope.com

Sample Checklist for New Business Professionals for their First 90 Days

Welcome and Congratulations on your decision to build your professional services business!

What do you need? Well, in order to market your business successfully, you will need to spend 20-25 hours a week building your social capital offline, and probably an additional 10 hours weekly, at least in the beginning, getting your online presence set up for success.

A Word about Your Budget

You'll need about $10,000 for a year of referral marketing and networking activities and another $5,000-$20,000 for online marketing activities (which might include a website). There's no limit to the amount of money you can spend on your marketing, but this is how much you are likely going to have to pay to play effectively in today's personal marketing world. A small investment when you think of the revenue that you will generate for yourself.

Your Personal Marketing Playbook

Time Frame	Offline Activities	✔	Online Activities	✔
By the end of Week One	Your office is set up and you have an address and phone number.	☐	You have a professional, full-colour headshot	☐
	You have a corporation (if that is necessary) and your banking is set up.	☐	You have developed your online marketing message for your website and LinkedIn platforms	☐
	You've developed a referral marketing message that tells the results you get, and for whom.	☐	You have selected and purchased the URL for your website	☐
	If you own a franchise, make sure all office administration requirements are completed	☐	Your email address is set up and your e-signature is developed	☐
	You've developed a one-year, three-year and five-year Personal Marketing Plan, for your business		You've included a one-year, three year and five-year online marketing plan for your business	
	Decide when your launch event is going to be	☐	You have commissioned a web designer and written copy for Home, About Us, & Services pages	☐
	Set up your personal marketing scorecard. Sample at YourPmp-Hope.com. Give a referral to a network member	☐	Provide a recommendation on LinkedIn to a member of your network	☐
	Watch for possible Saboteurs, like procrastination, that might keep you from moving forward	☐	Start looking for a videographer to work with you to develop some videos for your website	☐

Time Frame	Offline Activities	✔	Online Activities	✔
By the end of Week Two	Your CRM is set up for new business contacts	☐	You've set up an email marketing account through Constant Contact, Mail Chimp or HubSpot	☐
	You've stratified your network for current quality referral sources	☐	You've got a process for expanding your database in accord with anti-spam legislation	☐
	Your data base is fully prepared for your launch email and you've had your video shoot	☐	You've set up your Linked In profile and begun completing all sections	☐
	You've made a list of the places you are going to be networking, based on your target audience	☐	You have profiles on Twitter, FB, Google Plus, Instagram and Skype; you're connecting with people	☐
	Start using your scorecard. Give a referral to a member of your network.	☐	Set Google alerts for subject areas of relevance to your clients and network members	☐

Your Personal Marketing Playbook

Time Frame	Offline Activities	✔	Online Activities	✔
By the end of Week Three	First meeting with a Phase 3 member of your network	☐	You've listed potential blog topics, established an editorial calendar and drafted your first post	☐
	Practice your message, brainstorm on launch event venue sites (recruit members of your network to help you)	☐	Post to LinkedIn, Facebook and Twitter (if using all three) announcing your business services – include a call-to-action	☐
	Attend a networking event in your target market	☐	Connect on Linked In as appropriate with the people you met at the networking event	☐
	Hire a bookkeeper who is referral-minded	☐	Complete your content marketing/online strategy	☐
	Meeting with another Phase 3 member of your network	☐	Connect with the person you met with on Linked In as well as FB, Twitter and G+	☐
	Practice your message and brainstorm about your event with Phase 2 or 3 network members	☐	Spend two more hours working on your Linked In profile. Be sure to use a relevant background image.	☐
	Research venue sites for your launch event	☐	Video is proofed and finalized	☐
	Hire an event planner, if required	☐	Ensure Google Analytics will be enabled on your website and that you will have blog capabilities	☐
	Invest 15 hours weekly with network events, 1:1 meetings and other plays. Give a referral to a member of your network	☐	Complete proofing of copy for your website	☐
	Plan your week with your scorecard in mind and ensure you are increasing your points every month (See bookedsolid.ca for the score card)		Set up a free Hootsuite SM management account and schedule posts for FB, Linked In and Twitter to share articles found via your Google Alerts (two/week)	

Time Frame	Offline Activities	✔	Online Activities	✔
By the end of Week Four	Complete all administrative tasks	☐	Recommend three people from your network on Linked In	☐
	Research and shop for new networks, according to your target market	☐	Request three recommendations from your network on Linked In	☐
	Attend a networking event with your new network	☐	Connect on Linked In with the people you met at the networking event and spend one hour improving your Linked In profile	☐
	Meeting with a Phase 2 or 3 member of your network-practice your message	☐	Launch new website – invite everyone in your database to visit it	☐
	Brainstorm on event venue sites with network members	☐	Create a SM post asking your online network for recommendations for venue sites	☐
	Attend networking event-2-3 nights/week or more?—85% of life is just showing up	☐	Review your Google Alerts to identify more articles of value to members of your network	☐
	2 meetings with Phase 2 or 3 members of network	☐	Connect with Phase 2 and Phase 3 members of your network on Linked In, Twitter, FB and/or G+	☐
	Perfect your message, discuss your event with more members of your network	☐	Develop a list of informative videos you can create for your website and YouTube channel	☐
	Call selected network members (ensure personal connections)	☐	Send another informative and educational email blast to your network	☐
	Give a referral to a member of your network.	☐	Provide a Linked In recommendation to a valued member of your network	☐
	Spend 15 hours weekly on your plays, networking events and 1:1 meetings	☐	Connect with Phase 2 or 3 member of your network on Linked In, Twitter, FB and/or G+	☐
	Plan your weekly networking activities and s-t-r-e-t-c-h yourself		Draft a downloadable white paper and get it professionally designed	☐

Time Frame	Offline Activities	✔	Online Activities	✔
By the end of Week Five	Visit Venue Sites for Your Launch Event	☐	Check out reviews of the venue sites you visit online	☐
	Meet with a Phase 2 network member	☐	Connect with a Phase 2 member of your network on Linked In, Twitter, FB and/or G+—invite them to opt in to your database	☐
	Ask for help greeting guests at your event	☐	Support your referral sources on LinkedIn and other social media sites	☐
	Attend a networking event that is targeted to your ideal client	☐	Connect on Linked In with anyone you met at the networking event	☐
	Confirm venue and date of your own event	☐	Spend an hour improving your social media profiles	☐
	Meet with a Phase 2 member of your network	☐	Give a shout out to a Phase 2 or 3 network member on Linked In, Twitter, FB and/or G+	☐
	Give a referral to a member of your network	☐	Recommend a referral source through Linked In	☐
	Attend another new networking event	☐	Connect on Linked In with people you met at the networking event	☐
	Send out "save the date" e-blast to your network - Plan your list carefully according to 0,1,2,3 Relationship Phases	☐	Set up an "Event" on Facebook about your event and invite appropriate connections to attend	☐
	Confirm "Referral-Minded" Support Resources for your event	☐	Ask your network on Linked In for recommendations for people to support you at your event	☐
	Meet with Phase 1 or 2 member of your network	☐	Connect on Linked In with Phase 1 or 2 member of your network	☐
	Ensure you spend 18 hours weekly on your plays, networking events and 1:1 meetings	☐	Make sure you are drafting and posting blogs in accordance with your blog's editorial calendar	

Your Personal Marketing Playbook

Time Frame	Offline Activities	✔	Online Activities	✔
By the end of Week Six	Confirm all administrative and office details are completed	☐	Review your Google Analytics data; learning from that, adapt your blogging strategy if necessary	☐
	Meet with a Phase 2 member of your network	☐	Connect with a Phase 2 or 3 network member on social media; invite them in to your database	☐
	Attend a networking event. Give a referral.	☐	Connect on Linked In with people you met while networking—invite them to opt in to your database	☐
	Choose and execute a PMP play with 1 member of your network	☐	Support Phase 3 members of your network through retweeting or sharing some of their posts	☐
	Send out first invitations to your event launch, using event management software with registration capability	☐	Start working on a case study to showcase your expertise	☐
	Attend another networking event	☐	Connect on Linked In with the people you met networking—invite them in to your database	☐
	Participate in an activity with 4 people for at least 1 hour	☐	Post a picture from the activity on your social media profiles	☐
	Meet with a Phase 2 member of network to help with planning of your event	☐	Spend some time blogging; share the blogs you post on social media and with your dbase	☐
	Choose and Execute on a PMP play. Give a referral to a member of your network.	☐	Ask your webmaster to set up a landing page for the Irresistible Free Offer you will use to invite people in to your database	☐
	Meet with your coach	☐	Start drafting an Irresistible Free Offer for your website based on the biggest needs of your clients	☐
	Attend a Chamber of Commerce education event	☐	Tweet highlights from the event	☐
	Make sure your 0123 Relationship list is up to date	☐	Check registrations from Event registration site and set up an email database list with just those names on it	☐
	Start registration list for your event	☐	Give recommendations to three referral sources on Linked In; update your news feed	☐
	Give a second referral to a member of your network this week.		Schedule some of the articles selected for you by Google Alerts, as social media posts	

Your Personal Marketing Playbook

Time Frame	Offline Activities	✔	Online Activities	✔
By the end of Week Seven	Attend new networking event – join the group?	☐	Blog about your event, post it to Linked In and other SM sites	☐
	Phone calls to network to keep in touch ~*a good Friday habit!*	☐	Email invitations to your event to members of your network	☐
	Meet with Phase 1 member of your network with your Personal Profile Sheet	☐	Send out event invitations via emailing platform to your dbase	☐
	Give a referral to a member of your network	☐	Book a Skype call w. a member of your pre-vis. network; connect w. them on SM, invite them in to your dbase	☐
	Meet with Phase 1 member of your network	☐	Connect with Phase 1 members of your network on SM, and Like their Facebook Page, if they have one—invite them in to your dbase	☐
	Attend networking event		Connect on Linked In with people you met networking and comment on one of their Linked In posts	
	Participate in an activity with 4 people, at least 1 hour per person (golf, card or tennis game)	☐	Join a Linked In group related to your field and post a comment to one of the discussion groups in it	☐
	Give a referral to a member of your network.	☐	Connect with Phase 1 members of your network on SM—invite them to opt in to your database	☐
	Attend networking event	☐	Join five Linked In groups related to your field and post a comment to one of the discussion groups	☐
	Ensure that 18 hours weekly is dedicated to your plays, networking events and 1:1 meetings	☐	Research and choose a free online video prompter to use at your event	☐

204

Your Personal Marketing Playbook

Time Frame	Offline Activities	✔	Online Activities	✔
By the End of Week Eight	Invite a member of your network to an event	☐	Reach out to all members of your network via SM	☐
	Meet with a Phase 3 network member to discuss niche and event invitations	☐	Turn one of the blog posts you wrote into a PowerPoint presentation & post to SlideShare	☐
	Send out reminder invitations for your networking event	☐	Research online radio shows you might want to be interviewed for and contact the hosts	☐
	Give a referral	☐	Connect with Phase 2 or 3 network members on SM; invite them in to your dbase	☐
	Send out white paper with reminder reference to event	☐	Spend an hour working on your social media profiles	☐
	Attend a targeted networking event	☐	Connect with the people you met networking on SM—invite them in to your dbase	☐
	Meet with a Phase 2 or 3 network member to confirm participation	☐	Connect with Phase 2 or 3 network members on SM—invite them in to your database	☐
	Have 2 meetings with Phase 2 and 3 members of your network to plan participation at event	☐	Give recommendations to three referral sources	☐
	Attend a networking event	☐	Select more articles identified by Google Alerts for SM content curation, and schedule them	☐
	Give a referral to Phase 1,2, or 3 member of your network	☐	Spend an hour reviewing the group activity in your Linked In network and like, comment and share content as appropriate	☐
	Have an activity with 4 people	☐	Post a photo of your activity to your news feed if appropriate	☐
	Ensure that 18 hours weekly is dedicated to your plays, networking events and 1:1 meetings	☐	Check your Google Analytics to learn more about how people are arriving at and using your website	☐

Time Frame	Offline Activities	✔	Online Activities	✔
By the End of Week Nine	Plan your PMP activities (plan template is available at: YourPmp-Crossman.com YourPmp-Hope.com or	☐	Draft next blog, post it to your website; invite people to read it via SM & your emailing platform	☐
	Meet with a Phase 1, 2, or 3 member to help with your event	☐	Give recommendations to three referral sources	☐
	Attend a networking event	☐	Connect with the people you met at the networking event on social media	☐
	Meet with a Phase 1, 2, or 3 network member to plan event and encourage participation	☐	Spend an hour reviewing the news feeds of your Linked In network and like, comment and share content as appropriate	☐
	Give a referral	☐	Draft a quarterly newsletter and send it out via your mass emailing platform	☐
	Attend a new networking event	☐	Connect with the people you met while networking on SM	☐
	Meet with a 123 member	☐	Connect with a 123 network member on SM; like and share come of their posts	☐
	2 Meetings with 123 members to plan event and encourage participation	☐	Ask three members of your network for recommendations on Linked In	☐
	Participate in an activity with 4 people	☐	Post a photo of your activity to your news feed if appropriate	☐
	Give a high quality referral to a valued member of your network	☐	Connect on Linked In as appropriate with the people you met networking– invite them to download your IFO	☐
	Connect with 3 members of your network via phone or Skype	☐	Post your videos to your YouTube account and your website and invite people to view them via your SM accounts	☐
	Prepare advanced script for your event with input from your network	☐	Practise with your online video prompter to become comfortable using it	☐
	Ensure that 18 hours weekly is dedicated to your plays, networking events and 1:1 meetings	☐	Share a referral partner's content through your online properties	☐

Time Frame	Offline Activities	✔	Online Activities	✔
By the end of Week Ten	Make sure that you nail your event with event follow-up activities	☐	Draft another blog and post it to your website; use SM and an email blast to invite people to read it	☐
	Meet with a 123 member to plan event	☐	Support the 123 member by liking, commenting and sharing their posts online	☐
	Attend a networking event	☐	Connect on Linked In as appropriate with the people you met while networking – invite them to download your IFO	☐
	Meet with a 123 for education seminar set-up	☐	Post a picture of you and your 123 member, with their permission, to your SM accounts	☐
	Meet with a Phase 2 member to assist with event/education seminars	☐	Support the 123 member by liking, commenting and sharing their posts online	☐
	Give a referral to a new member of your network.	☐	Connect on Linked In with people you met networking– invite them to download free white paper	☐
	Send out email invitations to your network and include a link to an interesting white paper	☐	Post an invitation to your networking event via your social media platforms	☐
	Meet with a 123 member to assist with event/education seminars	☐	Check your Google Analytics account; learning from that, adapt your blogging strategy	☐
	Attend a networking event	☐	Connect on Linked with the people you met networking– invite them to download your free white paper	☐
	Confirm all final event details	☐	Post a note to your 123 members' social media accounts thanking them publicly for their assistance	☐
	Phone calls to network to confirm event participation and guests	☐	Select articles identified by Google Alerts and schedule them as social media posts	☐
	Ensure you're spending 20 hours weekly on your plays, networking events and 1:1 meetings	☐	Ask a Phase 3 network member to review your website and give you feedback on their experience of it	☐

Time Frame	Offline Activities	✔	Online Activities	✔
By the end of Week Eleven	Continue to develop your guest list	☐	Draft another blog, post it to your website, and invite people to read it via SM and your email platform	☐
	Regular phone calls with network members to ensure that guests will be coming	☐	Direct message or email people to set up conversations with prospects and referral sources	☐
	Group of 4 Activity – golf, cards, tennis	☐	Post an interesting aspect of your work day to social media	☐
	Make sure that you are well-rested and well-prepared when planning your event day	☐	Review your guest list and ensure you connect with all prospective attendees on Linked In	☐
	Prepare online tools to send thank you's to all guests	☐	Post a relevant question to each of your Linked In groups; monitor responses	☐
	Plan your Follow-up for your event	☐	Turn another blog into a PowerPoint presentation and post it to SlideShare	☐
	Meet with a 123; make a connection for a network member	☐	Support the 123 member by liking, commenting and sharing their posts online	☐
	Line up all tools for your event follow-up	☐	Invite a Phase 3 network member to write a guest blog for your website	☐
	Attend a networking event	☐	Update your status on social media and post a photo from the event you're attending with a caption honouring the hosts	☐
	Meet with a 123 – collaborate with them for your seminar offer	☐	Support the 123 member by liking, commenting and sharing their posts online	☐
	Phone calls to network to confirm guest list	☐	Ask Phase 3 network member if they have would like you to write a guest blog for them	☐
	Ensure you're spending 20 hours weekly on your plays, networking events and 1:1 meetings	☐	Post an invitation to your networking event via your social media platforms	☐

Time Frame	Offline Activities	✔	Online Activities	✔
By the end of Week Twelve	Plan your PMP activities	☐	Draft another blog; have someone look at it to ensure grammatical accuracy, then post it	☐
	Confirm outstanding event details	☐	Post an invitation to your event via your social media platforms	☐
	Send a reminder email about your event with an engagement program	☐	Select articles identified by Google Alerts and schedule them as social media posts	☐
	Work out script with speaker, and travel arrangements	☐	Send email to your event registrants thanking them for the registration, and telling them what to expect at the event	☐
	Meet with a new network member and invite them to your event	☐	Support the network member by liking, commenting and sharing their posts online	☐
	Meet with a 123 to help with guests at the event	☐	Support the 123 member by liking, commenting and sharing their posts online	☐
	Attend a networking event	☐	Post a photo of the event on SM along with a caption honouring event hosts	☐
	Meet with a 123 member of your network to ask for help with post-event education seminars	☐	Support the 123 member by liking, commenting and sharing their posts online	☐
	Attend a networking event; invite a new guest to attend with you	☐	Connect on Linked In with the people you met networking– invite them to download your free online resource	☐
	Attend a networking event	☐	Connect on Linked In with the people you met at the networking event – invite them to download your free online resource	☐
	Meet with a 123 to discuss event and post-event programs	☐	Support the 123 member by liking, commenting and sharing their posts online	☐
	Phone network members to see about their guest invitations	☐	Post an invitation to your networking event via your social media platforms	☐
	ENJOY YOUR EVENT!	☐	ENJOY YOUR EVENT	☐

PART SIX: CONCLUDING THOUGHTS

Concluding Thoughts

As you may have noticed when you reviewed the exhaustive list of plays, there are many, many options available to you for the development of your Personal Marketing Playbook. Your list of plays is unique to you.

And it is important to note that some plays that appealed to you would not be the same choice of plays made by other members of your network. Each to his/her own playbook!

The important idea is to keep working on your personal marketing, focusing on progress, rather than perfection.

Success comes from continued effort that is strategically directed towards the proven tasks that we know will work, time after time, business professional after business professional.

Do the work and you will reap the rewards.

The challenge is that many people who choose to become entrepreneurs are not always, by nature, consistency-oriented people. We love new ideas, we love learning new things and we are energized by possibilities – and not so much by repetitive action.

We fall prey to "Squirrel Syndrome," the tendency to become distracted by the next shiny bright idea that falls onto our horizon. It is all so exciting!!! If you see yourself in that description, know that you might turn out to be the biggest impediment to your own success and you are not alone.

A good coach will help you grow beyond your innate tendencies and allow you to see behavioral choices that will support your drive to success.

Being a professional services provider is not an easy road. It is an enormous amount of work. It takes an enormous amount of determination. Family members, partners, friends and others will not understand the path you are on and they may discourage you – intentionally or not -- from giving your business the time and energy it needs in order to thrive.

Stay the Course
The rewards are commensurate with effort. Stay the course, no matter what.

The objective of this book is to help you create a plan that includes activities or plays that will really motivate you, leveraging both referral and content marketing strategies, executed on and/or off line.

You are looking to create a Personal Marketing Plan that will grab you every day and direct you to the exciting activities that you *want* to do to grow your business and your network.

You Are Going to Grow
After all, if you are enjoying your business activities with members of your network who really resonate with you, you and your business are going to grow. Remember that it's almost impossible to succeed in any line of work without other people around you to support you to your success.

Making it Work
You need team members, accountability partners, mentors, advisors, cheer leaders and more in order to make this work.

If you are nervous about technology and all those "mysterious" ways the internet works, or if you simply don't like technology and the idea of using social media, may we invite you to consider all the ways it can serve you, rather than master you?

With any online activity, you are in charge of what you reveal. And, the more you learn about broadcasting your message, the more effectively you can manage your "online real estate" and start generating the revenue you desire.

215

It may not look easy, but adopting a learner's mindset will support you to generating the traction you need and, ultimately, put you in a position of choice over your online activity.

Remember to create a fresh personal marketing plan (PMP) every month as your relationships advance to the next level and as online opportunities evolve.

As mentioned, you may need a coach or accountability partner to help you keep on track — or more than one! Invest in your own success.

Last but not least, it is our hope that you will appreciate and cherish the real potential of your greatest asset: the people who surround and nourish you, your network.

For assistance with your online marketing efforts, please connect with Susan Crossman at susan@crossmancommunications.com.

You can also start a conversation with Susan and her team by filling out the questionnaire at https://survey.zohopublic.com/zs/myB0Jk

For assistance and accountability with your targeted referral networking and referral-building plans and activities , please connect with Paula Hope at paula@bookedsolid.ca.

About the Author – Susan Crossman:

Author Susan Crossman is an online marketing consultant, who helps her clients develop, manage, and leverage the web-related content they need to grow their business with clarity and authority.

She has an extensive background as a professional writer and marketer, and she is tenaciously focused on helping her clients untangle the often overwhelming task of showing up more powerfully online while leveraging the internet's vast possibilities for revenue generation.

You can visit her website at:
crossmancommunications.com

or email her directly at:
Susan@CrossmanCommunications.com

About the Author – Paula Hope:

Paula Hope is a sought-after referral marketing consultant, coach, speaker and trainer who helps talented business professionals become happily booked solid through referrals.

Paula has seen first-hand how powerful referrals can be in the corporate world and now, as a consultant focused on assisting professional service providers to exceptional success, she takes great delight in sharing her information with her clients.

You can visit her website at:
bookedsolid.ca

or email her directly at:
Paula@BookedSolid.ca

Manor House
905-648-2193
www.manor-house-publishing.com